ANTONIO CARLUCCIO
ITALIAN RECIPES

BOOKS FOR REAL COOKS

PAVILION

Pavilion Books for Real Cooks

Published in Great Britain in 1994 by
PAVILION BOOKS LIMITED
26 Upper Ground, London SE1 9PD

Recipes originally published by Pavilion in
An Invitation to Italian Cooking.

Design by Write Image
Jacket photograph © Gus Filgate

A CIP catalogue record for this book is available
from the British Library

ISBN 1 85793 393 1

Printed and bound by WBC Printers, UK

2   4   6   8   10   9   7   5   3   1

This book may be ordered by post direct from the
publisher. Please contact the Marketing Department.
But try your bookshop first.

CONTENTS

FOREWORD

Since I wrote my first cookery book, *An Invitation to Italian Cooking*, in 1986, awareness of Italian food has grown enormously. From the initial belief abroad that Italian cooking was solely represented by lasagne, pizza and spaghetti, the sheer diversity of Italian regional cooking has conquered great parts of the world – thanks also to the recent discovery that food cooked the Mediterranean way is terribly good for your health. At least fifty percent of the famous Californian cuisine is based on regional Italian cooking, and even French cuisine, so reluctant to take on board what is not French, has now adopted many Italian ingredients.

Why is Italian food so good? Pasta, for example, can be healthy, exciting, satisfying and easy to cook, all depending of course on immaculate ingredients and some imagination in preparing them. A steaming plate of freshly made tagliolini topped with a few slices of white truffle can be, in its remarkable simplicity, such an inebriating experience. Yet this dish would be only one part of an Italian meal which, for nutritional variety and pure pleasure, should be composed of at least three dishes: a little antipasto, a first course and a main course, all chosen to balance each other for taste, texture and consistency. A meal should be designed to satisfy both mind and body.

I learned to cook when I was a student, largely so that I could replicate the wonderful food prepared by my mother. She would go to great lengths to please each of us six children, as well as a demanding and critical father. Thirty-six years have passed since I left Italy and the memory of such meals have made me a man with a mission. I also had the good fortune of being born in the south and brought up in the north. This was my first asset in understanding the complexity of the food of the twenty Italian regions that make up Italian cooking.

I gained additional knowledge by visiting more than two thousand Italian restaurants in Europe during my twelve years in the business of selling wine. In most restaurants, the buying discussions were held in the kitchen which gave me an insider's view of the various types of cooking. The recipe collection in this book is a panorama of what I have experienced. In fact, to collect together all the Italian recipes, and all their variations, I would need to write twenty big cookery books. Perhaps one day I'll manage it.

With these recipes, I would like to transmit my passion for Italian food to you. Having tried almost every cuisine in the world, I am so convinced that Italian cooking is one of the best and most complete. I appreciate other kinds of cooking immensely, but never so entirely as I enjoy Italian food. That is why my mission has been to spread the gospel with books, with television, and with my restaurant.

My wife Priscilla and I are constantly researching ingredients and preparations from all the regions of Italy. Our specialist shop in London offers the very best of what we have found. Judging by its success, I would say that Italian food has become part of the British way of life, and is here to stay.

I hope you enjoy this book by trying and trying again. That is how I learnt.

Antonio Carluccio
London, November 1993

Antipasti

Acciughe Ripiene al Forno

BAKED STUFFED ANCHOVIES

Makes 12 'sandwiches'

24 fresh anchovies

1 tbsp chopped fresh dill

1 tbsp chopped fresh parsley

1 tbsp chopped fresh chives

1 tbsp chopped fresh rosemary

a few sage leaves, finely chopped

1 clove garlic, chopped

1 oz/ 25 g pine nuts, or chopped walnuts

2 tbsp olive oil

salt and freshly ground black pepper

a few drops of lemon juice

about ½ oz/ ⅓ US cup/ 10 g fresh bread crumbs

The fresh anchovy is undoubtedly one of the most popular fish in Italy. Each of the many coastal villages and cities has its own recipe, and rapid transportation means that even inland you can buy very fresh fish. In countries where fresh anchovies are not available, it's possible to use frozen ones instead: combined in this recipe with fresh herbs, they make a very unusual and appetizing dish. Fresh or frozen sardines offer another alternative, but since these are larger than anchovies, you will need only half as many.

Two anchovy 'sandwiches' per person make an antipasto; four would be sufficient for a main course.

METHOD

Preheat the oven to No 7/ 425°F/ 220°C. With a pair of kitchen scissors, cut off the head, tail and lower part of the fish, and discard the insides. Using your thumb, loosen the backbone from the flesh, leaving the two fillets still attached by the upper skin. Wash and dry the fish. Chop the herbs and garlic finely together and mix with the pine nuts and a tablespoon of olive oil. Grease a baking tray with a little olive oil and lay 12 of the anchovies skin side down next to each other on the tray. Spread a little of the herb mixture on each, season with salt and pepper, sprinkle with lemon juice and cover with another anchovy, skin side up, to make a 'sandwich'. Sprinkle with bread crumbs and pour on the remaining olive oil in a thin stream. Bake for 8–10 minutes until golden. Serve hot or cold.

Acciughe in Salsa Verde

ANCHOVY FILLETS IN GREEN SAUCE

Makes a 1 pint/ 500 ml preserving jar

12 oz/ 345 g can of anchovy fillets in oil

1 clove garlic

a large bunch of parsley

2 dried red chili peppers

the inside of a white bread roll, or 1 oz/ ⅔ US cup/ 25 g fresh bread crumbs

1 tbsp wine vinegar

enough olive oil to cover – at least ¼ pint/ ¾ US cup/ 150 ml

T his recipe, perhaps more than any other, reminds me of certain happy days of my youth when I would set out with my friends into the mountains or into near-by villages on outings which would invariably end in a small inn or café. Here we would consume vast quantities of anchovies in green sauce, slices of home-made salami and succulent fresh bread, all doused down with a locally produced Barbera wine. Few meals can surpass this excellent, if rustic, menu.

For this antipasto the ideal anchovies would be the salted kind that need soaking and filleting. However, this would cause the dish to be unnecessarily complicated, and equally good results can be obtained by using canned fillets in oil. Two or three fillets per person will be sufficient as a starter with fresh bread. The jar can be kept in the refrigerator and used whenever the occasion arises.

METHOD

Open the can of anchovies, and drain off the oil. Finely chop the garlic, parsley and chilis. Soak the bread in the vinegar, squeeze and finely chop. Mix these ingredients together. In a glass jar with a rubber seal, place first a layer of the herb mixture and then a layer of anchovies; cover with oil and press down. Repeat until the jar is full. Pour some olive oil over the top and keep in the refrigerator until required.

Cozze al Forno

MUSSELS AU GRATIN

1 lb/ 500 g fresh mussels
– about 12 per person

1 clove garlic, finely
chopped

2 tbsp finely chopped
parsley

salt and freshly ground
black pepper

2 tbsp dry bread crumbs
or 1 oz/ ⅔ US cup/
25 g fresh bread crumbs

1 tbsp olive oil

This recipe is popular in many Italian regions, and is a tasty dish that is relatively easy to prepare. It can also be served as a main course merely by increasing the quantity of mussels. Cooking the mussels with oil allows you to eat them hot or cold.

Try and choose the biggest and freshest mussels, making sure that they are tightly closed and are quite heavy.

METHOD

Clean the mussels under running tap water. Throw away any that are open or that float to the surface. Place the mussels in a lidded saucepan with a wineglass of water and bring to the boil. Shake the pan: the steam will open the mussels in a few minutes. (At this point throw away any that have *not* opened.) Put aside to cool.

Preheat the oven to No 7/ 425°F/ 220°C. Next, take off the top half of each shell. Loosen the mussels and arrange the lower shells one next to the other in a baking dish. Sprinkle them with the garlic and parsley mixed together, then with the bread crumbs, and season with salt and pepper. Finally pour a thin trickle of olive oil over each mussel. Then place the dish in a hot oven for about 10 minutes.

Insalata di Mare

SEAFOOD SALAD

🏛

A variety of fish can appear in this salad, preferably a shellfish of some kind, and some
prawns or shrimps. Squid, cuttlefish or octopus is
the essential ingredient, for both looks and texture.
All should be very fresh – frozen will not do.

METHOD

Scrub the mussels thoroughly, discarding any that
are open or have broken shells. Put a wine glass of
water in a saucepan with a lid, add the mussels and
steam them over a strong flame, shaking the pan
from time to time, for a minute or two. Put the pan
aside to cool, and then remove the mussels from
their shells. Clean the squid by removing the transparent bone and cutting off the head. Keep the tentacles whole in bunches and do not cut the body
at this point.

Bring a saucepan of water to the boil and add
some salt. Put in the squid, the prawn tails and the
scallops. The cooking time of all these fish is largely to do with their size, but should not take more
than 10–15 minutes: remove the prawn tails after
5 minutes; the squid, too (if they are small ones),
will be cooked in 5 minutes. Test for tenderness
and drain the fish when cooked. Cut the scallops
in half and large squid into ¾ inch/ 1.5 cm slices.
Cut the prawn tails into four. Mix the mussels
with the other seafood and leave to cool. Dress with
the lemon juice and olive oil, season with salt,
pepper and parsley and scatter the chives over the
top. Serve along with other antipasti as a light
summer main course.

SERVES 4

1 lb/ 500 g mussels in
their shells

¾ lb/ 350 g squid

6 oz/ 150 g giant prawns
(jumbo shrimp)

2 scallops weighing
about 5 oz/ 120 g
without shells

1 tbsp chopped parsley

a small bunch of chives,
chopped

the juice of a lemon

3 tbsp olive oil

salt and freshly ground
black pepper

Involtini di Prosciutto e Mozzarella

PARMA HAM AND MOZZARELLA FINGERS

Makes 24 involtini

12 slices of Parma ham

1 mozzarella

2–3 dried sage leaves, crumbled

1 tsp thyme

1 tsp dried rosemary

pepper

I really think this is the easiest recipe to prepare. It doesn't need to be cooked and it is ready in minutes. Wonderful for parties.

METHOD

Cut each slice of Parma ham in two halves. Cut the mozzarella first into thick slices and then into fingers. Chop the herbs finely together, making sure they are all mixed, then sprinkle the herbs over the mozzarella fingers. Roll each finger in a piece of ham and serve.

Funghi Ripieni

STUFFED MUSHROOMS

SERVES 4

F or this recipe you can use open cultivated mushrooms or field mushrooms. The stuffing need not be exactly as I suggest, but can be diversified according to your imagination and to the ingredients at hand.

METHOD

Preheat the oven to No 7/ 425°F/ 220°C. Clean the mushrooms. Detach the stalks and chop them coarsely. Prepare the filling: first beat the egg and add to it the chopped mushroom stalks, the chopped tomato, the roughly broken up bread, the Parmesan, chopped garlic, parsley, salt and pepper and finally 1 tsp olive oil. Mix well together and fill the mushroom cups with the mixture. Oil a baking dish and on it place the mushrooms side by side. Sprinkle the dry bread crumbs over the mushrooms and trickle with a little olive oil. Bake in a hot oven for 20 minutes until golden brown on top. Eat hot or cold.

4 large open mushrooms

1 egg

1 small ripe tomato, skinned and chopped

1 oz/ 25 g fresh bread

4 tbsp freshly grated Parmesan cheese

1 clove garlic, chopped

1 tbsp finely chopped parsley

salt and freshly ground black pepper

1 tbsp dry bread crumbs

3 tsp olive oil

Fiori di Zucchini Ripieni

STUFFED COURGETTE (ZUCCHINI) FLOWERS

SERVES 4
___

12 courgette (zucchini)
flowers
___

4 tbsp olive oil, for
frying
___

For the stuffing:
___

9 oz/ 1 ½ US cups/ 280 g
fresh ricotta cheese
___

salt and freshly ground
black pepper
___

3 grates of nutmeg
___

1 bunch chives, chopped
___

1 egg, beaten
___

4 tbsp freshly grated
Parmesan cheese
___

For the batter:
___

2 eggs
___

2 oz/ ½ US cup/ 50 g
flour
___

4 tbsp cold water
___

T his is above all a summer recipe, summer
being the time when these vegetables are in
flower. In Italy, especially, it is a well-known and
easily prepared dish, as the flowers are sold in all
the markets tied together with a willow branch.
Usually it is little old ladies who sell these flowers
in special baskets called *cavagne* along with herbs
and other garden produce. If you have no vegetable garden yourself, try to persuade a garden-
ing friend to let you have a few flowers.

METHOD

First make the batter. Beat the eggs, stir in the
flour evenly, then gradually add the water to make
a smooth consistency. Put it aside.

Meanwhile, clean the flowers carefully: gently
wash and dry the outside, and make sure there
are no insects inside. Prepare the filling by mixing
thoroughly together the ricotta, salt, pepper, nutmeg, chopped chives, beaten egg and the grated
Parmesan cheese. Use spoonfuls of this mixture to
fill the flowers. Then dip the flowers into the batter and proceed to fry in hot oil until golden-
brown. Drain on kitchen paper briefly before
serving.

Involtini di Melanzane

AUBERGINE (EGGPLANT) ROLLS

M y idea of aubergine rolls is a variation on the use of the vegetable in dishes alla parmigiana or al funghetto.

METHOD

Clean the aubergine and slice it lengthwise to a little less than ⅓ in/ 1 cm thick, sprinkle with salt and set aside for 10 minutes. Pat them dry. Preheat the oven to No 5/ 375°F/ 190°C. Heat the oil and fry the pieces on each side until golden in colour. Remove and leave to drain on kitchen paper. Coarsely chop together the parsley, pine nuts, capers and the garlic. Spread this mixture on the aubergine slices, roll each slice up and fasten with a toothpick. Place the rolled slices in a small baking dish and bake in a moderate oven for 25 minutes. Serve in a clean dish.

SERVES 4

1 large aubergine (eggplant) weighing about ¾ lb/ 350 g

olive oil for frying

1 tbsp parsley

1 tbsp pine nuts

1 tbsp capers

1 clove garlic

Insalata di Peperoni Arrostiti

ROAST PEPPER SALAD

SERVES 6

4 fleshy yellow and red
bell peppers

2 cloves garlic, coarsely
chopped

3 tbsp olive oil

1 tbsp coarsely chopped
parsley

salt

This recipe is an example of the way in which the flavour of the fleshy red and yellow bell peppers can change completely according to whether they are fried or roasted: the removal of the skin alters the taste of the peppers totally.

This is without a doubt one of my favourite recipes. It can be eaten either by itself, with some good wholesome bread, or as an accompaniment to meat dishes – especially pork.

METHOD

Roast the peppers over a charcoal grill (broiler), turning them frequently until black and blistered. Leave them to cool and then peel off the skin, which should come away quite easily if the peppers are well roasted. Remove the stalk and the seeds. Cut lengthwise into narrow strips and place in a dish, adding the coarsely chopped garlic. Dress with oil, parsley and salt. This dish can be eaten hot or cold, but improves with standing, and is excellent eaten the next day.

Insalata Capricciosa

RAW VEGETABLE SALAD

'Capricious' is quite an apt term for describing this salad, which can be used in many ways: in sandwiches, or as part of many antipasto dishes. It is particularly popular as a starter in Piedmont.

METHOD

The preparation is very simple. Simply peel the celeriac and the carrots and cut into matchsticks. Mix in the drained artichokes, cut into small strips, and the mayonnaise mixed with the extra lemon juice, and season with salt and pepper.

To make the mayonnaise, stir the egg yolks together in a heavy bowl, then slowly add the olive oil dribble by dribble. Stir continuously until you have added all the oil: the mayonnaise will become very thick and sticky. At the end stir in the lemon juice which should liquefy the sauce a little. Season with salt and pepper.

8 small pickled artichokes (carciofini) in oil

4 oz/ 100 g celeriac

4 oz/ 100 g carrots

2 tbsp mayonnaise (see below)

juice of half a lemon

salt and freshly ground black pepper

Mayonnaise

2 egg yolks

9 fl oz/ 1 US cup/ 250 ml olive oil

juice of half a lemon

salt and freshly ground black pepper

Peperoni Gialli con Bagna Cauda

YELLOW PEPPERS WITH BAGNA CAUDA

SERVES 4

———

2 fleshy yellow bell
peppers

For the bagna cauda:

8 cloves garlic

———

¼ pt/ ⅔ US cup/ 150 ml
milk

———

a nut of butter

———

20 anchovy fillets in oil

———

Even though Piedmont has no sea coast, anchovies play an important part in local gastronomy. Indeed, there is a valley in the province of Cuneo where the villagers occupy themselves exclusively with the conservation of this fish in salt. Of the many recipes using anchovies, this is certainly one of my favourites: the distinctive flavour of the bagna cauda is juxtaposed with the sweet taste of the roasted peppers. This dish is also excellent served cold.

METHOD

Clean the peppers, remove the stalks and seeds, and cut them into quarters. Put the cloves of garlic in a pan with the milk and cook gently until soft for about 35 minutes. Meanwhile, preheat the oven to No 7/ 425°F/220°C. Throw away most of the milk, add the nut of butter and the anchovies and let the mixture slowly dissolve over a low heat until a paste is produced. Pass it through a sieve. Place the pepper pieces on a greased dish and put them in the hot oven for 15 minutes. Remove from the oven and turn the heat down to No 5/ 375°F/ 190°C. Fill each piece of pepper with some of the paste and put back into the oven for a further 15 minutes, until the peppers go brown at the edges.

Zucchini alla Scapece

FRIED COURGETTE (ZUCCHINI) SALAD

T his is a typically Neapolitan method of dressing not only cooked greens and other vegetables but also anchovies. Aubergines (eggplants) make an equally tasty alternative to the courgettes suggested here. The origin of this dish is not quite certain, but is probably derived from the Spanish or Provençal escabeche, which means to dress with a marinade of oil, vinegar and spices. It is an excellent appetite-teaser.

METHOD

Slice the courgettes ¼ in/ 5 mm thick and fry them, a few at a time, in hot oil in a pan until they are a good brown colour on both sides. Remove them from the pan, place them in a dish and sprinkle with salt. Tear the mint leaves off the stem and scatter them whole among the courgettes. Add the oil and vinegar and then the pieces of garlic, and mix well together. Leave to marinate for at least a couple of hours before serving to allow the flavours to develop fully.

SERVES 6

2 lb/ 1 kg courgettes (zucchini)

salt

oil for frying

a bunch of fresh mint

2 tbsp olive oil

1 tbsp wine vinegar

1 clove garlic, sliced coarsely

FIRST COURSES

Brodo di Pollo con Cappelletti

CAPPELLETTI IN CHICKEN BROTH

T his is a slightly richer version of the traditional pastina in brodo or fine spaghetti in
broth which can be found on the menu of most
Italian restaurants and which can be made with a
great variety of fine pasta such as stelline, tubettini, biavette, etc. The cappelletti owe their name to
their resemblance to hats and can be hand-made
if you happen to possess a great deal of patience.
If this is not the case, I would heartily recommend
that you buy them from a good Italian delicatessen,
naturally paying attention to the 'sell-by' date.
The best cappelletti to buy are probably those
sold in a hermetically sealed pack and of recent
manufacture. This type of pasta is a speciality of
Bologna and of the Emilia Romagna region. However, they are also popular in most other areas of
Italy. The Piedmontese and Lombards, however,
seem to prefer raviolini, which are similar to the
cappelletti in taste but not in shape.

SERVES 4

2 pint/ 1 litre chicken or
beef stock

4 oz/ 120 g dried
cappelletti or raviolini,
or 7 oz/ 200 g fresh
cappelletti

1 oz/ ¼ US cup/ 30 g
freshly grated Parmesan
cheese

METHOD

Bring the stock to the boil and add the cappelletti or raviolini. Bring back to the boil and simmer
until the pasta is cooked: this should take about 15
minutes for dried and about 10 minutes for fresh
pasta. Serve in a warm plate with the addition of
a little Parmesan cheese grated on top.

Crema di Funghi Porcini

WILD MUSHROOM SOUP

SERVES 4

1 lb/ 500 g fresh ceps, or
alternatively 1 lb/ 500 g
field mushrooms plus
1 oz/ 25 g dried ceps

1 medium onion, finely
chopped

4 tbsp olive oil

2 pint/ 1 litre beef stock

4 tbsp double (heavy)
cream

salt and freshly ground
black pepper

For the croûtons:

a nut of butter

2 slices white bread

S imply handling the main ingredients for this soup – wild mushrooms – fills me with ecstasy and reminds me of autumnal walks in beautiful woods in search of them. This soup can be made in two ways, both of which are delicious. In the Neal Street Restaurant I serve the version made with fresh ceps, and it has become one of the most popular items on the menu in the autumn. (During the rest of the year I make it with ceps I have frozen.) The alternative version is even simpler and (unless you have gathered your own ceps) cheaper. You could even make an exception and, for once, use a bouillon cube for convenience.

METHOD

If you are using fresh ceps, clean them and cut them into pieces. Cook the finely chopped onion in the oil for 3–4 minutes, then add the ceps and sauté them for 6–7 minutes. Add the stock, bring to the boil and simmer for 20 minutes. (If you are not using fresh ceps, soak the dried ones in luke-warm water for 10 minutes. Meanwhile, fry the field mushrooms together with the onions and then add the soaked ceps with their water and the stock. Simmer for about half an hour.) To finish either method, take the pan from the heat and blend the contents. Then return the soup to the pan, add the cream, salt and pepper and heat slowly. Remove from the heat before it boils, and serve hot. To make croûtons, merely cut the bread into little cubes and fry in butter so that they become crisp and golden.

Zuppa di Pesce

FISH SOUP

his recipe of mine is merely a version of one of the hundreds of fish soups that can be found in all Italian coastal towns. It is a dish that can be tasty even if you have only a couple of kinds of fish to choose from. Monkfish, prawns (shrimps) and even mussels are ideal for this soup as they have a good flavour and do not disintegrate when cooked. For an even tastier soup you may well wish to include some heads of the larger fish. If you increase the proportions of fish, this soup can even become a main course.

METHOD

Put the oil in a large pan and fry the shallot together with the carrot and the celery until the onion becomes golden and soft. Pour in the wine, bring to the boil, and allow it to evaporate for 1 minute. Add the fish and the stock and simmer for 20 minutes. Remove the heads and shells from the prawns and shell the mussels, and return their flesh to the soup. Lightly rub the clove of garlic over the toast and place one slice in the bottom of each soup bowl. Pour in the soup and serve straight away.

SERVES 4

4 tbsp olive oil

1 shallot or onion, chopped

1 carrot, chopped

1 celery stalk, chopped

half a glass of dry white wine

8 prawns (shrimp)

20 mussels

½ lb/ 250 g monkfish cut into pieces, or substitute scallops for the monkfish

3 pints/ 1.5 litres fish stock

4 slices of buttered toast

1 clove garlic

salt and freshly ground black pepper

Zuppa di Cardo con Polpettine

CARDOON SOUP WITH DUMPLINGS

SERVES 4

3 pints/ 1.5 litres meat broth

1 cardoon weighing about ¾ lb/ 350 g

7 oz/ 200 g minced (ground) beef

tbsp finely chopped parsley

4–5 grates of fresh nutmeg

1 tbsp freshly grated Parmesan cheese

1 egg

1 tbsp dry bread crumbs

salt and freshly ground black pepper

The cardoon is a member of the artichoke family and is a speciality of the Piedmont region, where it is mainly eaten in Bagna cauda. It is a very versatile vegetable with a slightly bitter taste. The centre near the root of the cardoon tends to be particularly bitter, so cut this out before cooking.

Last summer when I was exploring the province of Alessandria I came across a whole field of cardoons which were being specially treated to blanch them. This is done by tying them and half-burying them underground up until the first frost. Normally, only the inside of the plant is eaten, this being the most tender. Here is the recipe that my mother used to prepare with this vegetable.

METHOD

Wash the cardoon and chop it into pieces about 1 in/ 2 cm thick, then put them to cook in the meat broth until they are tender – about 20 minutes. Meanwhile, into a bowl put the meat, parsley, nutmeg, Parmesan cheese and bread crumbs and add the beaten egg and the salt and pepper. Knead this mixture thoroughly so as to obtain a smooth paste. Shape this with your hands into little dumplings and put them to simmer in the hot broth for about 10 minutes. Serve hot with a light sprinkling of Parmesan cheese if you so wish.

MINESTRONE

SERVES 4

T his soup is well known by its Italian name throughout the world. The name derives from minestra, meaning a soup. (In many parts of Italy minestra means green.) Normally this is prepared with whatever leftover vegetables are to be found in the kitchen, and so to list the precise ingredients needed for a minestrone would be nonsensical, even dictatorial! Almost all the different regions in Italy have their own typical minestrone, which will then be suffixed 'alla milanese', 'alla genovese', 'alla piemontese', etc.

Perhaps the most practical hint for you to follow is that the fine flavour of Parma ham is essential to the success of this dish. You can ask for bits and pieces of prosciutto from your Italian grocer or delicatessen, for example, the skin, the pieces cut out from around the bone and the tail-end piece.

3 pints/ 1.5 litres water

a total of 3 lb/ 1.5 kg vegetables, made up of any or all of the following: carrots, celery, courgettes (zucchini), cauliflower, potatoes, fresh peas, beetroot (beet), garlic, leeks, Brussels sprouts, parsnips, marrows (squash)

1 small onion

8 tbsp olive oil

14 oz/ 400 g can borlotti beans (if you can find fresh ones, so much the better)

some fresh basil leaves, or 1 tsp dried basil

a good ½ lb/ 250 g prosciutto scraps

2 small tomatoes, skinned

4 tbsp freshly grated Parmesan cheese

METHOD

Heat the oil in a large saucepan. First fry the chopped onion, then add the prosciutto pieces and the water, letting this simmer for an hour. Meanwhile, clean the vegetables and chop into cubes. Discard the prosciutto pieces and add the other vegetables of your. choice, as well as the drained beans. Add the skinned tomatoes after a further 20 minutes. Cook for at least a further 30 minutes, after which time you should taste to see that all the vegetables are cooked, particularly the carrots. Then add the basil and serve piping hot. Minestrone is also a delicacy when eaten cold. Freshly grated Parmesan should be served separately.

Pasta all'Uovo

BASIC PASTA DOUGH

Makes 1 lb/ 450 g pasta dough

10 oz/ 2 ½ US cups/ 300 g Farina OO or plain white (all-purpose) flour

3 large, very fresh eggs

generous pinch of salt

I talian cooks use a great deal of imagination combining pasta with local produce, ending up in many cases with really superlative dishes. For the most part these dishes have been created with hand-made pasta, and some people still consider that this more than repays the considerable time and energy spent in its making. My mother turned this laborious task into a social event: a number of her friends would sit gossiping round the large table while she rolled out her fusilli.

In recent years a multitude of pasta-making machines has appeared on the market. I have tried out nearly all the different types and have come to the conclusion that unless you wish to make enormous quantities of pasta, the greatest help is given by the simplest of hand-driven machines which allow you to produce dough of different thicknesses and to cut the pasta into strands of different sizes. Here, however, I'll describe the process of making pasta by hand.

The ideal proportions are one large egg to every 4 oz/ I US cup/ 100 g of flour (see p. 128), but variations in temperature and humidity as well as in the ingredients themselves may produce slightly different textures, and you may need to vary the quantity of flour slightly: the thing to aim for is a dough which has been kneaded until it is perfectly smooth and elastic, yet firm.

METHOD

Pile the flour in a volcano-shaped mound on a spacious work surface – ideally of marble. Break the eggs into the centre and add some salt. Stir the eggs into the flour, with a fork at first and then with your hands, until it forms a coarse paste: add a little more flour if the mixture is too moist.

At this stage you may bring a pasta-making machine into play. Otherwise, it's a good idea at this point to clean your hands and the work surface before you start kneading the dough. Lightly flour the surface and your hands, and knead the dough with the heel of your hand, pushing it away from you and folding it back towards you, one hand at a time. Flour the surface and your hands from time to time while you work. After about 10–15 minutes the dough should be smooth and elastic.

Allow the dough to rest for 15–30 minutes before rolling it out. Once again, dust the surface and the rolling pin with flour. Roll the dough gently, working away from you, and rotating the dough by a quarter-turn so that it remains circular.

The thickness to aim for should be ³⁄₁₆ in/ 2 mm for ravioli and cappelletti and ³⁄₈ in/ 4 mm for lasagne and cannelloni. If you are making stuffed pasta such as ravioli, don't allow the sheet of dough to dry, but proceed to incorporate the filling as instructed in the appropriate recipes. If you are simply making lasagne or cutting strips of noodles, place a clean towel on the work surface and leave the pasta on it to dry for about half an hour, letting different sections of it hang over the edge in turn. Then fold the sheet of pasta into a loose roll on the work surface and cut it into ribbons of the desired width. Open out the rolls of noodles gently and allow them to dry for a further 10 minutes or so before cooking.

Cook pasta in a large saucepan, preferably with a rounded base. Use plenty of boiling water: the general rule is 2 pint/ 1 litre water and 1 tsp salt to every 4 oz/ 100 g pasta. When you put the pasta into the pot, give it a quick stir to prevent it from sticking together. (It is only with lasagne, which must be immersed one sheet at a time, that it is

necessary to add a few drops of oil to the water.)
Cooking time varies according to the kind of pasta,
its thickness and whether it is stuffed, but home-
made noodles and ribbons will take about 3–5
minutes. Stir the pasta while it is cooking, preferably with a long wooden fork. Always test the
pasta when you think it should be almost done: it
is ready when it is al dente, and slightly resistant.
A little before it reaches that stage, take the
saucepan off the heat, add a glass of cold water, and
leave for a couple of seconds. Then drain the pasta
and return immediately to the saucepan or a pre-
heated dish, mixing it with a little sauce and perhaps some grated cheese. Serve it immediately.

COLOURED PASTA

Pasta can be bought in different colours. Often the
colouring is a gimmick, for visual effect, with the
exception of green pasta based on spinach: check
the packet to make sure that the colouring is not
artificial.

Here are some suggestions for making your
own coloured pasta by adjusting the proportions
in the basic recipe to incorporate a colouring ingredient. The resulting dough should have exactly the
same consistency and texture, but you may find
that these adulterated doughs are slightly more

Green Pasta
***

12 oz/ 3 US cups/ 350 g
flour
***
3 eggs
***
3 oz/ 80 g cooked
spinach
***
salt
***

tricky to knead and harder to roll out into thin
sheets. You may sometimes have to add a little
extra flour to stiffen the dough.

For green pasta, the spinach should be cooked in
a little water, drained very thoroughly and finely
puréed. You may need a little extra flour to stiff-
en the dough. Here the colouring makes a subtle
contribution to the flavour.

Use a juicer or a food processor to obtain the juice, which will colour the dough a deep mauve.

Purple Pasta

14 oz/ 3 ½ US cups/ 400 g flour

2 eggs

6 tbsp beetroot juice

salt

The tomato paste introduces a slightly acid flavour into the pasta.

Red or Pink Pasta

14 oz/ 3 ½ US cups/ 400 g flour

3 eggs

2 tbsp tomato purée

salt

The quantity of flour is reduced and unsweetened cocoa powder substituted. This kind of pasta is often served in Italy together with game sauce.

Brown Pasta

13 oz/ 3 ¼ US cups/ 380 g flour

4 eggs

2 tbsp bitter chocolate powder

salt

You will need the ink from one large or two small cuttlefish to colour the black pasta for four servings. The ink sac, which is a silverish tube shape about 4 in/ 10 cm long and ¾ in/ 2 cm in diameter, is found at the extreme bottom of the body. Be careful to withdraw it intact. Mix the thick black substance, the ink, with water to make 100 ml of liquid. Take care not to make this dough too soft.

Black Pasta

14 oz/ 3 ½ US cups/ 400 g flour

2 medium eggs

¼ pint/ ½ US cup/ 100 ml dilute cuttlefish ink

Tagliatelle con Carciofi

TAGLIATELLE WITH ARTICHOKES

SERVES 4 AS A MAIN COURSE

4 fresh and tender small artichokes

juice of half a lemon

2 large ripe tomatoes or 4 small ones

4–6 spring onions (scallions), chopped

3 tbsp virgin olive oil

2 tbsp white wine

salt and freshly ground black pepper

2 tbsp chopped parsley

1 lb/ 450 g home-made tagliatelle, 14 oz/ 400 g dried tagliatelle

2 oz/ ½ US cup/ 60 g freshly grated Parmesan cheese

I t is a typically Sienese habit to bring together artichokes and pasta. I came across this combination of tagliatelle and artichokes in a small trattoria in Siena where I was once eating. I was so impressed by this distinctive taste that I have no trouble at all reconstructing it here. For this dish you will need particularly small artichokes.

METHOD

Clean and trim the artichokes retaining only the bottom and the most tender leaves. Cut into slices and put in a bowl of water with lemon juice to prevent oxidization.

Peel the tomatoes and cut into chunks. Fry the chopped spring onions in the olive oil and almost immediately add the artichokes and tomatoes; cook over a moderate flame for 10–15 minutes or until the artichokes are tender. Then add the wine and simmer for another 5 minutes, season with salt, pepper and the parsley.

Cook the tagliatelle as usual, drain and mix in half the sauce. Serve in warm plates with the remainder of the sauce and with grated Parmesan cheese sprinkled on top.

Tortelloni di Magro
MEATLESS TORTELLONI

The word 'magro' means that the filling is based on vegetables and cheese and does not contain any meat. It is a very light and tasty dish which I wouldn't hesitate to recommend to all vegetarians. Accompany this dish with a fresh wild salad, and you will have a lovely summer meal. If, however, you add a meat sauce, you can make a more substantial main-course dish.

The essential ingredients are ricotta, which is a very low-fat cheese, and herbs, which can be varied according to their availability. I have made this dish with such herbs as mint, basil, coriander, chives, parsley, and either a little Swiss chard or its substitute, spinach.

METHOD

Clean and cook the chard or spinach leaves, drain well and squeeze out excess water, then finely chop. Make the filling by mixing together the chopped chard or spinach, the crumbled ricotta, the herbs, Parmesan cheese and salt and pepper. Prepare the pasta as in the basic recipe and roll it out as thinly as possible. To make the tortelloni, cut the pasta in 2 in/ 5 cm squares. Place a little of the filling in the middle of each square and fold over the pasta to make triangular parcels. Press together the edges to firmly seal each triangle. Then roll around a finger and press the ends together to form the circular tortelloni. Boil this pasta as usual and add to it a little melted butter and serve with extra Parmesan cheese at the table.

SERVES 4

1 lb/ 450 g pasta dough (see basic recipe)

For the filling:

8 oz/ 250 g Swiss chard or spinach leaves

5 oz/ ⅔ US cup/ 150 g fresh ricotta

1 tbsp chopped mint, or other herbs

4 tbsp freshly grated Parmesan cheese

salt and freshly ground black pepper

For serving:

2 oz/ 4 tbsp/ 60 g butter

2 oz/ ½ US cup/ 60 g freshly grated Parmesan cheese

Pasta e Fagioli

PASTA WITH BEANS

SERVES 6

2 lb/ 1 kg fresh borlotti beans (with their skins); or ½ lb/ 250 g dried borlotti or cannellini beans; or 2 medium cans of unsalted borlotti beans

2 celery stalks, finely chopped

4 tbsp virgin olive oil

2 cloves garlic

4 oz/ 100 g prosciutto trimmings, chopped into small cubes

2 medium potatoes, cut into cubes

3 ripe tomatoes, skinned and chopped, or a medium can of peeled plum tomatoes, chopped in the can

1 red chili pepper, chopped

4 oz/ 100 g tubettini or mixed pasta

10 fresh basil leaves

2 pints/ 1 litre stock

salt and freshly ground black pepper

This is one of the rare pasta dishes that enjoys equal popularity in all the different Italian regions. Apparently the best version of this dish is to be found in Naples, where scraps of pasta from the ends of different packets are mixed with spaghetti, which is crushed into spoon-sized pieces prior to cooking.

The best flavour is obtained by using fresh borlotti beans, which are admittedly slightly hard to come by in markets abroad. In Italy they are commonly found in the shops and markets around the month of August and are recognizable by their green and reddish colour. If you are unable to find the fresh variety you can also use the borlotti beans that are found in cans. Another excellent substitute are white cannellini beans (well favoured by the Neapolitans) which are smaller than the borlotti ones but very tasty.

Whenever I go for the first time to a new Italian restaurant I usually order pasta e fagioli in order to get an idea of the cook's skill. Indeed, because it is a dish that is easy to prepare, many cooks do not give it much of their attention and end up by completely spoiling one of the more famous rustic pasta meals.

METHOD

If you are using dried beans leave them to soak in water the night before you use them. Then boil them in some unsalted water for 2–3 hours until they are tender. If you are using fresh beans boil these for 30–40 minutes until they are cooked. Of course, if you are preparing the dish with canned beans, there is no need to precook these, and they can be drained and added directly to the sauce.

Fry the chopped celery and the chopped prosciutto in a large saucepan in the olive oil over a medium flame. After a few minutes, add the chopped potatoes and chili, stirring to prevent the prosciutto from browning. After about 10 minutes add the finely chopped garlic and cook it for a couple of minutes before adding the tomatoes. Wait a further 10 minutes before adding two-thirds of the drained beans, but keep the remainder of these aside to be reduced to a mash and added to thicken the sauce. Pour in the broth or the water and bring to the boil. Now add the pasta and after 10 minutes, add the basil leaves and the mashed beans. Season with salt and pepper.

When serving you may find that pouring a trickle of olive oil over the dish greatly enhances the flavour. You can also place a basil leaf on top as a decoration.

Gnocchetti Sardi con Broccoli

SARDINIAN GNOCCHI WITH BROCCOLI

SERVES 4

1 lb/ 500 g broccoli tips (cooked weight)

2 oz/ 60 g smoked bacon, finely chopped

4 tbsp olive oil

3 cloves garlic, sliced

½ pint/ 1 US cup/ 200 ml milk

14 oz/ 400 g Sardinian gnocchetti

a little hot water from cooking the pasta

2 oz/ ½ US cup/ 60 g freshly grated Parmesan cheese

salt and freshly ground black pepper

Another recipe that I have created is based upon the combination of Sardinian gnocchetti, made by the firm De Cecco, and greens. It has the advantage of being absurdly easy to prepare. If, for any reason, you cannot obtain calabrese or broccoli, you can substitute cauliflower, though the former is preferable for the distinct taste and colouring it gives to the sauce.

METHOD

Clean the broccoli tips, then boil them in some lightly salted water until they are soft (about 12–15 minutes). Drain them, chop finely and then put them to one side. Take quite a large pan and start to fry the chopped bacon in the olive oil. Once it begins to brown, add the slices of garlic, which should not be allowed to colour. Next add the chopped broccoli and the milk and cook for 10–15 minutes over a high flame, stirring every now and again. At the end of this time the broccoli should be reduced to a creamy texture.

Cook the gnocchetti for 12–15 minutes until they are al dente, drain (reserving a little of the water), then pour into the pan with the broccoli mixture, adding the Parmesan, salt and pepper. Add a spoonful or two of cooking water so that the mixture is creamy rather than stiff. Stir well over a moderate flame for a few minutes or so, and serve in warm dishes.

Trenette col Pesto

TRENETTE WITH PESTO SAUCE

14 oz/ 400 g trenette

For the pesto sauce:

1 clove garlic

2 fistfuls fresh basil leaves

1 oz/ 25 g pine nuts

4 tbsp grated pecorino picante

4 tbsp grated Parmesan cheese

¼ pint/ ½ US cup/ 100 ml olive oil

salt

he true home of the classic pesto sauce is in Liguria, where the ingredients needed can be obtained all the year round. There are many different variations of this sauce, which is always accompanied by the large flat spaghetti called trenette, or also by home-made pasta shapes called trofie.

In summer when basil is in season and abundant, it's worth making a large enough quantity of pesto to freeze. Out of season, however, when you can come by only a couple of fresh basil leaves, I suggest you use them to 'improve' a jar of bought pesto.

METHOD

Chop the basil leaves roughly and slice the garlic. In your pestle, grind the garlic to a paste, add the basil leaves and pound until they begin to break up. Add the pine nuts and as you pound them, they will begin to amalgamate with the basil. At this point, slowly start to dribble in the olive oil; when the sauce has become liquid, add the pecorino and Parmesan cheese, stir in well and season with salt. How much salt depends on the type of pecorino cheese you have used. Some can be very salty.

Cook the trenette in salted boiling water until al dente (about 8 minutes).

Gently warm half of the sauce, but do not boil. Dilute the sauce with 2 or 3 spoonfuls of the pasta cooking water. Drain the trenette and mix well with half the sauce. Distribute on serving plates and add the other half of the sauce on top. Sprinkle with Parmesan or pecorino. Decorate with a fresh basil leaf.

Festoni del Ghiottone

GOURMET LASAGNA

SERVES 8 AS A MAIN COURSE

For the meatballs:

10 oz/ 300 g minced (ground) meat

1 clove garlic, finely chopped

1 tbsp chopped parsley

good 1 oz/ 6 tbsp/ 30 g freshly grated Parmesan cheese

2 medium eggs

1 ½ oz/ 1 US cup/ 40 g fresh bread crumbs, soaked in a little milk and then squeezed dry

salt and freshly ground black pepper

oil for frying

T his dish reminds me above all of those interminable Christmas meals where succulent course follows succulent course. As it requires quite a lot of preparation work, I would recommend that you only attempt to make it on important occasions. Because festoni is such a rich and substantial dish, you may wish to make it a main course, accompanied only by salad.

METHOD

Preheat the oven to No 6/ 400°F/ 200°C.

Make a paste by mixing the minced meat, the finely chopped garlic, parsley, Parmesan cheese, eggs and the soaked bread crumbs. When you have thoroughly stirred this mixture and added some salt and pepper start shaping from it little walnut-sized meat balls which you then fry in oil until they are of a golden colour.

Prepare the sauce by frying in fresh oil the chopped onion; when it is only half-cooked, add the chopped chicken liver. When these ingredients are cooked (after about 3 minutes) you can add the chopped tomatoes and continue to simmer for about half an hour over a low heat. Towards the end of this time, add the fresh basil leaves, the salt and the pepper.

Cook the pasta for 5–7 minutes or until it is al dente, drain, then add some of the sauce so that it is all coated. Take a deep baking tin and start making the timbale by spreading a layer of sauce over the bottom on to which you arrange some of the cooked festoni. Next on top of the pasta place some of the sliced salami, some meat balls and some slices of fontina cheese. Cover these with another 3 or 4 spoonfuls of sauce and a sprinkling of Parmesan cheese. Repeat this procedure until you have used up all the ingredients. When you have reached the final layer of fontina, pour on the well-beaten eggs, which will bind the pasta together. Over this pour the last of the sauce and the Parmesan cheese.

Put the tin in the oven for 25 minutes. When ready, leave the dish for 5 minutes before dividing into portions with a knife and serving hot. You will find the washing up involved in this recipe quite considerable but it is more than justified by the end result.

For the sauce:

4 tbsp olive oil

1 medium onion, chopped

4 oz/ 100 g chicken livers, washed, dried and chopped

2 large cans of peeled tomatoes

5 basil leaves

salt and freshly ground black pepper

For the layers:

1 lb/ 500 g festoni

4 oz/ 100 g spicy Neapolitan salami, sliced

10 oz/ 300 g fontina cheese, sliced

3 oz/ ⅔ US cup/ 80 g freshly grated Parmesan cheese

4 medium eggs, beaten

Bucatini alla Carbonara

BUCATINI WITH BACON, EGGS AND CREAM

SERVES 4

14 oz/ 400 g bucatini

7 oz/ 200 g pancetta affumicata (in one piece)

3 tbsp olive oil

2 egg yolks (preferably free-range eggs)

2 whole eggs

4 tbsp double (heavy) cream

2 oz/ ½ US cup/ 60 g freshly grated Parmesan cheese

salt and freshly ground black pepper

S ome people say the name carbonara is derived from the Carbonari, those revolutionaries who before 1861 worked to unify Italy. Somebody else says carbonara derives from coal.

Wherever it comes from, whoever cooked it for the first time had a brilliant idea: the use of uncooked eggs yolks as a sauce. In the recipe use Barilla's spaghetti no. 7 (fairly thick) or bucatini, spaghetti with a hole through it.

METHOD

Remove the skin and little bones from the piece of pancetta. Cut into ½ in/ 1 cm strips. Put a large saucepan of water on to boil. Beat the egg yolks with the eggs, add the cream, a pinch of salt (this depends on how salty the pancetta is) and the grated Parmesan.

Heat the olive oil in a pan and fry the pieces of pancetta, turning them over until they become golden and slightly crisp.

Put the bucatini into boiling salted water; it will take about 8–10 minutes to cook, then drain it. Use the water you drain from the pasta to heat your serving bowl. Mix the drained bucatini with the pancetta and the hot oil from the pan. Put into your heated serving bowl and mix together with the egg, cream and Parmesan mixture. Season and serve immediately with additional Parmesan at the table.

Risotto

BASIC RISOTTO METHOD

C hoose Carnaroli, Arborio or Vialone rice (see p. 130), which will cook to the right consistency for a good risotto. Use a heavy saucepan with a rounded bottom to prevent the rice from sticking in the corners. It should be big enough to contain the rice, plus the liquid (broth or stock and wine) that will be slowly added to it, increasing the volume by as much as three times. The spoon for stirring must be a wooden one. The heat must be moderate and constant. The stock must be kept simmering to avoid interruption of the cooking process; keep this pan next to the risotto pan.

Carefully coat the rice in the initial butter or oil before adding any liquid and turn the rice in the pan with a wooden spoon. You start to add the boiling stock when the rice is well and truly impregnated with butter and starts to stick to the bottom of the pan. Add only as much hot stock at a time as the rice calls for – that is, not too wet and drowning the rice, but enough to see the grains gradually absorbing the liquid as they cook – about a ladleful at a time. Continue to stir and add the stock until the rice is cooked (20–25 minutes).

At this stage remove the pan from the heat and, without stirring, let the rice absorb the last liquid. The risotto should have a creamy consistency, but still be firm to the bite. Taste for seasoning and serve straight away, stirring in (with the exception of seafood and champagne risottos) a knob of butter and the freshly grated Parmesan cheese. This last operation is called *mantecare*, possibly from the Spanish manteca which means butter.

Risotto con Porcini

MUSHROOM RISOTTO

SERVES 4

about 12 oz/ 300–350 g
firm small fresh ceps, or
fresh button mushrooms
plus 1 oz/ 25 g dried
ceps

1 small onion, finely
chopped

2 tbsp olive oil

1 oz/ 2 tbsp/ 30 g butter

12 oz/ 350 g Arborio rice

3 pints/ 1.5 litres chicken
stock, or water plus
2 bouillon cubes

salt and freshly ground
black pepper

a further nut of butter

2 oz/ ½ US cup/ 60 g
freshly grated Parmesan
cheese

T his dish is popular throughout northern Italy,
especially in Piedmont. Together with truffle risotto, it is my favourite dish. (I know: 'Yet
another!' you say to yourself, only this time it is
true, for it combines both an excellent flavour and
my favourite hobby of picking and eating wild
mushrooms.) Faced with the perennial problem of
finding fresh ceps in generous quantities, you can
use ordinary mushrooms plus a few dried porcini
for extra taste. But this risotto is also eminently
suitable for those wild mushrooms that you have
gathered in season and then frozen.

METHOD

Gently clean the ceps or other mushrooms, using
a sharp knife and a brush (avoid washing them
whenever possible). If you are using dried ceps, put
them to soak in a small bowl of water for 15 minutes. Meanwhile, slice the fresh ceps or mushrooms. Finely chop the onion and fry in the oil and
butter. When the onion begins to colour, add the
sliced ceps and continue to fry over a moderate
flame for a couple of minutes. If using the dried
ceps, chop them into small pieces and add to the
mushrooms, keeping the water they soaked in to
add to the risotto later with the stock. Add the
rice and proceed according to the basic risotto
method (p. 39).

When the rice is al dente, remove from the
heat, season, and stir in the nut of butter and the
Parmesan cheese. Serve hot, if you like decorating
each portion with a slice of mushroom.

Risotto con Asparagi

ASPARAGUS RISOTTO

O ther vegetable risotto dishes can be prepared along the lines of this asparagus recipe. Use any other vegetable that when slightly overcooked dissolves into a creamy substance ideal for a risotto: broccoli, spinach, artichokes, marrow (squash), courgettes (zucchini), cauliflower. To enhance the flavour of the rice, recycle the water in which you cook the vegetables. These risottos are perfect for vegetarians.

1 lb/ 500 g fresh green asparagus (weighed, cleaned and trimmed)

3 pints/ 1.5 litres water (for cooking asparagus and for risotto)

2 bouillon cubes (you can buy vegetarian ones)

1 small onion, thinly sliced

2 oz/ 4 tbsp/ 60 g butter

12 oz/ 350 g Arborio rice

2 oz/ ½ US cup/ 60 g freshly grated Reggiano Parmesan cheese

salt and freshly ground black pepper

METHOD

Wash and peel the asparagus and cut away 1 good inch/ 3 cm or so of the hard white stalk at the bottom (use this and the skin to add flavour to the cooking water). Cut off about 2 in/ 5 cm of the tips and set them aside (as they are tender they will need less cooking) and keep them intact for decoration. Boil the asparagus stalks with the skins and scraps in 3 pints/ 1.5 litres water to which you have added the stock cubes. When they are half-cooked add the tips. When fully cooked strain the stock and keep it simmering. Separate out the asparagus tips and stalks. Set the tips aside for decoration, but chop the stalks finely.

Fry the onion in half the butter, then add the chopped asparagus and toss it for a couple of minutes. Now add the rice and proceed as for the basic risotto method (p. 39), adding the broth until the rice is al dente and creamy but not too solid with asparagus sauce. Remove from the heat and wait for a minute or two, then stir in the remaining butter and the freshly grated Parmesan cheese. Serve in bowls and decorate with asparagus tips.

Risotto alla Milanese con Luganega

SAFFRON RISOTTO WITH SAUSAGE

SERVES 4

10 oz/ 300 g luganega pork sausage, or fresh minced (ground) pork meat

optional: salt, freshly ground black pepper and 4 grates of nutmeg to season fresh pork

1 small onion, chopped

2 oz/ 4 tbsp/ 60 g butter

2 tbsp olive oil

half a glass of dry white wine

12 oz/ 1 ¾ US cups/ 350 g Arborio rice

3 pints/ 1.5 litres beef broth, or water plus 2 bouillon cubes

2 sachets powdered saffron, or 2 pinches saffron strands

4 oz/ 1 US cup/ 100 g grated Parmesan cheese

A ny rice dish that is described as 'milanese' usually contains some saffron. Saffron rice is in itself a very delicate dish; the addition of lugane-ga turns it into something rather more substantial, which can even be served up as a main course. Luganega is fresh pork sausage that is sold by length (its name derives from the Greek 'lukani-ka'). This typically Lombardian or Milanese prod-uct was usually made in the winter months when the household pig was killed. Nowadays, howev-er, this sausage can be found all the year round. It is recognizable by the fact that it is made in a very long intestine of about 1 ¼ in/ 3 cm in diameter. I suggest you substitute fresh pork if you can't obtain luganeghe.

METHOD

Remove the sausage skin and break the meat into pieces, or, if you are using fresh pork, season it with pepper, salt and nutmeg.

Fry the finely chopped onion in half the butter and the oil, added the sausage meat or the seasoned minced pork. After the onion has turned golden and the meat has browned, add the wine which you should let evaporate for a couple of minutes before pouring in the rice. You start to add the stock when the rice has absorbed all the butter and oil and when it begins to stick to the pan. Proceed now as for other risotto dishes (p. 39), adding the salt, pepper and saffron as you progress.

When the rice is nearly cooked, incorporate the rest of the butter and half of the cheese. Serve on dishes with more grated cheese on top.

Risotto alle Erbe

HERB RISOTTO

T his is a deliciously refreshing dish which is particularly suitable for meals in late spring when many varieties of herbs can be found and when, if the weather permits, meals may be eaten outside. It is not necessary to restrict yourself to the herbs mentioned here – use whichever fresh herbs you please. However, don't attempt this dish using dried herbs.

METHOD

Lightly fry the chopped onion in half the butter over a moderate flame. Add the rice and proceed according to the basic risotto method (p. 39), adding stock as needed. Meanwhile, chop the herbs and the walnuts with a knife and squeeze or crush the garlic. When the rice is half-cooked, add the chopped herbs, walnuts and garlic. When the rice is cooked, add the Parmesan and the rest of the butter. Add salt and pepper to taste and serve straight away.

SERVES 4

1 small onion, chopped

2 oz/ 4 tbsp/ 60 g butter

12 oz/ 1 ¾ US cups/ 350 g Arborio rice

3 pints/ 1.5 litres chicken stock

at least 8 tbsp finely chopped fresh herbs chosen from: mint, coriander, rosemary, sage, parsley, dill (use sparingly), basil, oregano, tarragon, thyme

10 walnut halves

1 clove garlic

2 oz/ ½ US cup/ 60 g freshly grated Parmesan cheese

salt and freshly ground black pepper

Polenta con Funghi

POLENTA WITH WILD MUSHROOMS

SERVES 4

For the sauce:

1 small onion, chopped

3 tbsp olive oil

1 oz/ 2 tbsp/ 30 g butter

12 oz/ 350 g fresh ceps,
or field mushrooms plus
scant 1 oz/ 25 g dried
ceps

1 small can peeled plum
tomatoes

6 fresh basil leaves

salt and freshly ground
black pepper

For the polenta:

3 pints/ 1.5 litres salted
water

10 oz/ 1 ¾ US cups/
300 g yellow polenta
flour, or 1 packet 13 oz/
2 ¼ US cups/ 370 g
Valsugana polenta

1 oz/ 2 tbsp/ 30 g butter

2 oz/ ½ US cup/ 60 g
freshly grated Parmesan
cheese

T his recipe reminds me of outings into the mountains made in my youth, invariably finishing up in some trattoria or other, where polenta with mushrooms would always be on the menu, especially in the autumn. The memory of this polenta which would be prepared in a large copper pot over a wood fire makes my mouth water even today. For the ceps, which are usually quite hard to come by, you may substitute ordinary field mushrooms combined with a few dried ceps to give flavour.

METHOD

Clean and slice the mushrooms and soak dried ceps for 10 minutes in lukewarm water. Prepare the sauce by frying the chopped onion in the oil and butter, followed by the sliced mushrooms. Cook these two ingredients together over a high flame for 10 minutes, then add the liquidized tomatoes and continue cooking for another 20 minutes so that the water from the tomatoes evaporates. When everything is fully cooked, add the salt and pepper and basil leaves.

Bring the salted water to the boil, then very carefully add the polenta flour stirring constantly with a wooden spoon so that no lumps appear. You must continue to stir the polenta until you see that it starts to come away from the side of the saucepan. This will take only 5 minutes if you are using quick polenta, 30 minutes if you are using polenta flour. When this happens, add the butter and the grated Parmesan cheese, stirring all the time until you see that all the ingredients have melted and are thoroughly mixed with the polenta. Serve directly in heated shallow bowls, pouring some sauce into the middle of each and sprinkling some Parmesan cheese over the top.

A much richer polenta, like they make in the Aosta valley, can be obtained by adding to the mixture another 70 g butter, 40 g Parmesan and 100 g Fontina cheese cut into cubes. Naturally polenta can be used with various kinds of sauce-based ragoûts and is also terrifically good cold, cut into slices and either grilled or fried in butter.

Pizza alla Napoletana

NEAPOLITAN PIZZA

**To make 4 pizzas 11 in/
27 cm in diameter**

For the dough:

1 ¼ lb/ 5 US cups/ 600 g
Farina OO or plain white
(all-purpose) flour

1 ½ oz/ 45 g compressed
yeast (or the equivalent
quantity of dried yeast
powder or granules: see
maker's instructions)

a pinch of salt

16 fl oz/ 2 US cups/
300 ml warm water

2 tbsp olive oil

For the sauce:

2 tbsp olive oil

1 clove garlic, chopped

12 ripe plum tomatoes,
skinned and halved or
1 large can plum
tomatoes, chopped in
the can

T his classic pizza is both one of the simplest to
prepare and the most tasty. In Naples it is
customary to eat pizza in one's hands.

METHOD

Dissolve the yeast in the warm water to which
you have added the salt and olive oil. Pour the
flour into a mound on a clean working surface
and make a hole in the centre of it. Add the yeast
mixture drop by drop into the centre of the flour,
mixing with your hands until all the liquid is
absorbed, forming large lumps. Knead the dough
with your hands until it has a smooth texture,
then roll it into a ball. A good pizza depends on the
quality of the dough used.

Next, sprinkle some flour into a large tin or
dish and place the dough in it, spreading a little oil
over the top to prevent a crust from forming.
Cover the bowl with a dry linen cloth and leave to
rise for 1 hour in a warm place – not less than
68°F/ 20°C. After this time the dough should have
increased in volume by three times.

Now begins the preparation of the pizza proper. Preheat the oven to No 8/ 450°F/ 230°C. Rub
the four 11 in/ 27 cm pizza pans with olive oil.
Flour the working surface. Divide your dough
into four and roll each into a ball. (It is better not
to use a rolling pin but to ease the dough by gently pressing out the dough with the plump part of
your hand, the heel of your thumb and with your
fingers.) Starting from the middle, smooth the
dough out to a thickness of about ¼ in/ 6 mm.
I suggest you make the edges slightly thicker to

prevent the topping from running away, and this method of rolling leaves the characteristic round edge which should go crisp in the oven.

Place each pizza on an oiled pizza pan.

Spread on each circle of dough 2 spoonfuls of the combined tomato sauce. Sprinkle this with the oregano. Pour a trickle of olive oil over the top and place in a very hot oven for about 10–15 minutes, until you see the edges become a golden-brown colour.

For the topping:

2 tsp dried oregano

4 tbsp olive oil

salt and freshly ground black pepper

Focaccia al Rosmarino

PIZZA BREAD WITH ROSEMARY

SERVES 8–10

For the dough:

2 lb/ 8 US cups/ 1 kg flour

3 oz/ 75 g fresh yeast, or the equivalent amount of dried or powdered yeast

4 tbsp olive oil

20 fl oz/ 3 US cups/ 600 ml water

2 tsp brown sugar

For the topping:

3 tbsp fresh rosemary leaves

coarse salt and freshly ground black pepper

4 tbsp olive oil for the top and the baking tray

T o breakfast off a delicious piece of freshly baked focaccia will immediately lift you out of even the foulest of moods when you have got out of bed on the wrong side. Professional bakers (who make bread in their shops) in Genoa and throughout Italy also usually sell delicious focaccia. The most common variety that is produced is merely topped by some oil and salt and it comes in large rectangular shapes which are then cut into slices. It can also be made, however, in the shape of a pizza. The focaccia should be slightly thicker than a normal pizza as it is very similar to bread in consistency and like bread it can accompany all sorts of food. Chopped into pieces it can be consumed with aperitifs.

METHOD

Prepare the dough as described in the recipe for pizza alla napoletana and roll it out until it is either a rectangle or a circle 1 in/ 2 cm thick: this amount of dough makes one big rectangular pizza about 14 × 20 in/ 35 × 50 cm. Place it on an oiled baking tray. Preheat the oven to No 8/ 450°F/ 230°C.

Prick the dough all over with a fork then dribble with olive oil, scatter the rosemary leaves, generously grind fresh pepper and finally sprinkle salt over the whole surface. Bake in the very hot oven for 20 minutes: the top should be golden, but the rosemary must not brown.

Pizza Marinara

PIZZA WITH ANCHOVIES, TOMATOES AND GARLIC

The combination of garlic, oregano, basil and anchovies with the addition of tomatoes has always been synonymous with Italian food. When eating this classic pizza, you certainly will recall some good things on holiday in Italy. This classic is equally good hot or cold.

METHOD

Make the pizza dough as in the recipe for pizza alla napoletana and leave to rise for 1 hour. Preheat the oven to No 8/ 450°F/ 230°C.

In the meantime, make the tomato sauce. Fry the sliced garlic in hot olive oil, add the chopped tomatoes almost immediately and leave to simmer for 15 minutes. Season with salt, pepper and 4 fresh basil leaves torn into pieces.

Press out the dough to make 4 pizzas and lay them in oiled pizza pans. Spread each pizza with tomato sauce, place 6 anchovies on each pizza, scatter the chopped garlic over the surface and then the oregano. Tear the basil leaves into small strips and place them amongst the anchovies. Dribble the olive oil over the whole surface and season with freshly ground pepper – no salt, as the anchovies provide sufficient. Bake the pizza in a hot oven for 10 minutes. Serve hot or cold.

Makes 4 pizzas

dough made with 1 ¼ lb/ 600 g flour (follow basic recipe as for Neapolitan pizza, p. 46)

24 anchovy fillets

1 tbsp oregano

4 cloves garlic, finely chopped

8 fresh basil leaves

8 tbsp olive oil

freshly ground black pepper

For the tomato sauce:

1 medium can chopped Italian tomatoes

2 tbsp olive oil

1 clove garlic, sliced

salt and freshly ground black pepper

4 fresh basil leaves

Pizza con Pancetta Affumicata

PIZZA WITH ITALIAN SMOKED COOKED BACON

iii

MAKES 4 PIZZAS

dough made with 1¼ lb/ 600 g flour (see basic recipe)

10 oz/ 280 g pancetta affumicata (buy it in one piece)

12 oz/ 350 g smoked mozzarella

12 small green preserved peppers

salt and freshly ground black pepper

4 tbs olive oil

I f you imagine that pizza is nothing more than freshly baked bread, remember the topping can be as varied as you wish. In this case a bacon and cheese bread. The wonderful smoked pancetta, which is obtainable from most Italian delicatessens, combined with the smoked mozzarella and the contrasting element of those little preserved green peppers is a balance of tastes making something very appetizing indeed.

METHOD

Make the dough as in the recipe for pizza alla napoletana and leave to rise for 1 hour. Preheat the oven to No 8/ 450°F/ 230°C.

Press the dough out into your oiled pizza pans.

Cut the pancetta into small pieces ¼ × ¾ in/ 5 mm × 2 cm. Slice the smoked mozzarella. Cut the small green peppers into 2 or 3 pieces. Scatter the pancetta pieces on to each pizza, dot with the slices of mozzarella cheese. Place the bits of green pepper in between the slices of cheese. Generously grind over black pepper, sprinkle with salt. Finally dribble over olive oil and bake in the hot oven for 8–10 minutes. The cheese should melt and the pancetta become slightly golden. Serve hot.

FISH

Carpa Impanata e Fritta

CARP IN BREAD CRUMBS

SERVES 4

4 pieces of carp
weighing a total of
about 1 ¾ lb/ 800–900 g
when cleaned

1 clove garlic, crushed

2 tsp olive oil

2 eggs, beaten

2 tbsp chopped parsley

salt and freshly ground
black pepper

flour for dusting

about 4 oz/ 1 US cup/
100 g dry bread crumbs

oil for frying

1 lemon for garnish

When I was living in Vienna I used frequently to visit a restaurant near the Danube which specialized in cooking carp that was caught locally. The secret of the success of this restaurant lay almost entirely in the superb flavouring and texture of the bread crumbs with which the carp was covered.

METHOD

Gut the carp under running water, remove the large hard scales and then cut the flesh from the bones so that you have 2 large fillets, one off each side of the fish. Cut each fillet into two. Crush or squeeze the garlic and add the juice to the olive oil. (Alternatively, use olive oil in which you have soaked for at least a few days some peeled cloves of garlic.) Beat the eggs and add the garlic oil, the parsley, salt and pepper. Dust the carp pieces in flour, dip them in the egg mixture and then cover them in bread crumbs.

Heat about ½ in/ 1 cm oil in a large pan until hot, but not smoking; fry the pieces of carp gently until the bread crumbs are golden and the fish is cooked. Depending on the thickness of your pieces of carp, they should be cooked after 15 minutes of frying. Serve garnished with pieces of lemon and accompanied by a basil, tomato and onion salad.

Trota Allo Zenzero

TROUT WITH GINGER

G inger is a root which has a particularly strong flavour, especially when it is fresh. Although it is most used in Eastern cooking, Italians also favour it in their more exotic dishes.

METHOD

Gut and clean the trout under running cold water, and dry each one carefully with a cloth. Salt inside and outside and then moisten the fish with milk. Roll them in the flour so that they are lightly dusted.

Heat the butter in a large heavy pan and when it fizzes add the trout and fry gently over a medium flame until golden on both sides. The fish should be cooked in 15 minutes. Remove them from the pan and keep warm in a serving dish. Cut the ginger into matchsticks and chop the spring onions. Fry the ginger in the butter in same pan, increasing the heat, and almost immediately add the spring onion and the lemon juice. Stir all together just for a minute, season with salt and pepper, then pour this sauce over the trout. Serve immediately.

SERVES 4

4 trout weighing ½ lb/ 250 g each or 2 trout weighing 1 lb/ 500 g each

salt

4 tbsp milk

flour for dusting

3 oz/ 5 tbsp/ 75 g butter

a walnut-sized piece of fresh ginger root, cut into matchsticks

1 bunch spring onions (scallions), chopped

the juice of a lemon

freshly ground black pepper

Tortiera di Acciughe

BAKED ANCHOVIES WITH OREGANO

SERVES 4

1 ¾ lb/ 800 g fresh anchovies

3 tbsp olive oil

1 clove garlic, finely chopped

1 tsp oregano

the juice of a lemon

2 tbsp dry bread crumbs

salt

This is a typical dish from Naples where it is called either Tortiera or 'anchovies au gratin'.

You will need some fresh anchovies (alternatively, if these are hard to come by, small sardines will do). I have tried using frozen anchovies with quite a good result. In the chapter on antipasti I have already described several ways of preparing anchovies: this is another simple yet tasty recipe.

METHOD

Preheat the oven to No 6/ 400°F/ 200°C.

Clean and fillet the anchovies. To do this, cut off the head and tail, open the fish along the stomach and gently pull out the backbone with your thumb and finger. You will thus obtain two fillets joined together by the skin of the back. Grease a flat baking tray with a little of the olive oil. Lay in it the anchovies skin side down, as close as possible to one another, but not overlapping. Scatter the chopped garlic and the oregano over the anchovies, sprinkle with the lemon juice, then cover with a light layer of bread crumbs. Trickle over the bread crumbs the remainder of the olive oil, season with salt and then place the tray in the oven for 7–8 minutes. Once the bread crumbs are golden-coloured and crisp, the fish will be ready. Serve immediately with a mixed salad and some good bread.

Fritto Misto di Pesce

MIXED FRIED FISH

SERVES 4

½ lb/ 250 g squid

½ lb/ 250 g peeled prawns (shrimp)

½ lb/ 250 g whitebait (smelts)

plenty of flour for dusting

olive oil for deep frying

salt and freshly ground black pepper

2 lemons

One of the first dishes that I order whenever I set foot in an Italian seaside town is the fritto misto di pesce. I am sure that everyone who has visited Italy at one time or another will have tried this speciality which combines the most tender and delicate Mediterranean fish, and includes shellfish, small soles, squid and any other fresh and tender creatures from the sea – the result inevitably reminds one of good weather and the holidays.

This dish can be found almost anywhere on the coast of Italy as any combination of ingredients may be used.

METHOD

Shell the prawns if necessary. Wash the whitebait and leave to dry. Clean the squid and cut the body into rings; if they are small, leave the tentacles whole in their bunches. If they are large, cut them into smaller pieces. Thoroughly toss all the fish in plenty of flour, shaking off any surplus. Heat the olive oil in a deep fryer (or a large saucepan), and immerse the fish in it a few at a time. Cook until they have turned golden in colour, drain carefully on kitchen paper and arrange on a large serving dish. Sprinkle with salt and pepper, and decorate with pieces of lemon.

A good rocket salad will complete this excellent meal.

Coda di Rospo Allo Zafferano

MONKFISH WITH SAFFRON SAUCE

SERVES 4

about 1 ¾ lb/ 800 g
monkfish, cleaned
weight

1 onion

1 celery stalk

1 small carrot

salt

1 oz/ 2 tbsp/ 25 g butter

3 tbsp white flour

7 fl oz/ 1 US cup/ 200 ml
good fish stock

2 tbsp white wine

2 grates of nutmeg

1 sachet saffron

salt and freshly ground
black pepper

8 parsley sprigs

A lthough this fish looks very ugly (in the shops you will only find the edible part, that is to say the tail, on sale) it has quite a firm flesh which is absolutely delicious. Indeed, if monkfish is cut into chunks and fried with bread crumbs, it can easily be confused with prawns. Monkfish can be roasted, boiled or grilled.

This recipe describes a simple yet sophisticated way of cooking monkfish.

METHOD

Clean the fish, removing the bones and skin, then cut into serving-size pieces. Make a court bouillon with 2 pints/ 1 litre of water, the celery, carrot and onion. Poach the pieces of monkfish in the court bouillon, without allowing it to boil, for about 15–20 minutes.

Meanwhile, prepare the sauce. Heat the butter in a saucepan, and when it fizzes, add the flour; stir well and allow to cook, not brown, for about 5 minutes. Heat the fish stock in a separate saucepan. Slowly add the hot stock to the flour and butter, stirring all the time; finally add the wine, the saffron and the nutmeg, continue to stir and cook gently for a further 10 minutes. The sauce should be neither too runny nor too thick. Season with salt and pepper to taste.

To serve place 2 or 3 spoonfuls of sauce on to your heated plates, put the monkfish on to the sauce and decorate with sprigs of parsley. Accompany this dish simply with boiled potatoes and green beans in butter.

Filetti di Sogliole con Canterelli

FILLET OF SOLE WITH CHANTERELLES

I t is not a widespread practice in Italy to serve fish with mushrooms. Indeed, this particular recipe came to me in England, where there is an abundance of wild mushrooms and where one may also purchase the famous Dover sole. I have chosen to use the very delicate chanterelle mushroom to complement the delicate flesh of this fish. This recipe can also be made with black Horn of Plenty (*Craterellus cornucopioides*) and Mousseron mushrooms.

METHOD

Clean the carrot and cut in half. Wash the celery stalk. Fill a fish kettle with water to 2 ½ in/ 6 cm. Put in the carrot, onion, celery, peppercorns, bay leaf and salt and bring to the boil. Meanwhile, roll up each sole fillet and secure with a wooden cocktail stick. When the court bouillon is boiling, add the rolled fillets, then reduce the heat to barely simmering and poach for 10–15 minutes. The moment the sole are cooked remove from the court bouillon and put aside and keep warm.

Clean the chanterelles with a brush, only washing them if really necessary. Slice the onion finely and chop the garlic into small pieces. Heat the butter in a large frying pan and fry the onions; when they begin to turn in colour add the garlic, and after a minute the chanterelles. Keeping the heat up high, fry the chanterelles, stirring gently. Then add the wine and continue to cook until most of the liquid has evaporated. Stir in the cream and season with salt and pepper. Pour the chanterelle sauce over the fillets of sole and serve immediately.

SERVES 4

1 ½ lb/ 750 g sole fillet

For the court bouillon:

1 carrot

1 celery stalk

1 bay leaf

1 small onion

1 tsp peppercorns

salt

For the chanterelle sauce:

½ lb/ 250 g chanterelle mushrooms

4 oz/ ½ US cup/ 115 g butter

1 small onion

1 clove garlic

half a glass of dry white wine

2 tbsp double (heavy) cream

salt and freshly ground black pepper

Trance di Rombo Lesso con Salsa Piccante

TURBOT WITH A PIQUANT SAUCE

SERVES 4

4 slices turbot, each weighing about 7 oz/ 200 g

For the court bouillon:

3 pints/ 1.5 litres water

2 or 3 bay leaves

1 small onion, cut in half

1 tsp peppercorns

1 carrot, thinly sliced

For the piquant sauce:

½ pint/ 1 ¼ US cups/ 300 ml milk

salt

2 oz/ 50 g butter

½ oz/ 15 g plain flour

3 tbsp dried tomato paste

5 anchovy fillets (cut into small pieces)

salt

a pinch of cayenne

2 tbsp double (heavy) cream

T urbot is one of the most delicate and sought-after fish, which is also usually big enough to be cut into slices. Whether it is roasted, poached or stewed, turbot still keeps its immaculate white colour and delicate taste. Owing to this delicate flavour it may be combined with a variety of different ingredients for an excellent result.

In this recipe I have chosen to poach the turbot and to accompany it with a spicy sauce. Turbot should always be eaten with boiled potatoes.

METHOD

Bring the court bouillon to the boil. When boiling furiously, turn the heat right down, add the slices of turbot and cook very, very gently for 10 minutes.

To make the sauce, heat the milk to hot, not boiling. Melt the butter in a small saucepan, add the flour and stir with a wooden spoon for 3 or 4 minutes to cook the flour – but don't let it brown. Stir in the tomato paste and the pieces of anchovy. Break up the anchovy with the spoon in the pan as you start to add the hot milk, a little at a time, stirring to form a smooth cream.

Season with salt and cayenne pepper and stir in the cream at the end. Place the slices of turbot on individual hot plates and pour the piquant sauce over them. Serve with boiled new potatoes and a salad of mâche.

Tonno alla Siciliana

TUNA SICILIAN STYLE

T una fish is commonly found in Sicily, where many tales are narrated about the tonnare – fishing trips organized to trap whole shoals of huge tuna fish which are then pulled up into the boats, not without some risk on the part of the fishermen. The tonnare expeditions are considered a kind of ceremony in Sicily and the fish are not only tinned but also eaten fresh, cooked in a variety of ways.

The meat of tuna fish is very substantial and is usually cut into slices so that it may be either fried, grilled or, as in this typical recipe, stewed.

METHOD

Salt the steaks and then dust them with flour on both sides. Slice the red peppers into strips. Chop the garlic finely and skin and roughly chop the tomatoes.

Heat the olive oil in a large frying pan and, when hot, fry the steaks briefly on both sides just to seal in the juices. Remove them from the pan and reduce the heat. Put the red pepper in the frying pan and fry gently for 6 or 7 minutes, then add the garlic. Cook the garlic with the pepper for just a few minutes – they must not brown. Add the tomatoes, olives, rosemary, bay leaves, oregano and crushed chili. Stir the ingredients together, add the Marsala and return the tuna fish steaks to the sauce. The sauce should cover the tuna fish. Simmer gently for a further 15–20 minutes with the lid on the pan. The tuna should be tender, but the sauce should remain fresh-tasting. Season with black pepper and more salt if necessary and serve immediately.

SERVES 4

4 steaks fresh tuna, weighing about 7 oz/ 200 g each

flour for dusting

salt

4 tbsp olive oil

For the sauce:

2 cloves garlic, sliced

1 red pepper

4 tomatoes, skinned and chopped

20 black olives

2 bay leaves

1 sprig of rosemary

a pinch of oregano

1 dried chili pepper

1 small glass of dry Marsala

freshly ground black pepper

Pesce in Casseruola
———
FISH CASSEROLE

SERVES 4
———

½ lb/ 250 g large fresh
prawn tails (jumbo
shrimp)
———

½ lb/ 250 g very small
squid
———

1 lb/ 450 g red mullet:
4 small fish, if possible
———

1 carrot
———

a large handful of tender
celery leaves
———

1 shallot
———

4 tbsp olive oil
———

1 tsp fennel seeds
———

½ pint/ 1 ¼ US cups/
300 ml fish stock
———

The principle behind this recipe is a useful one: it doesn't bind you to specific fish, though you should have a mixture of three or more different kinds. Money can also dictate your choice of ingredients – you can include crustaceans from lobster to shrimp, shellfish from scallops to clams, and red mullet or any fish with firm flesh.

METHOD

Clean the squid just by removing the transparent bone and cutting off the head; leave the body and the tentacles intact.

Clean and scale the red mullet. Slice the carrot finely and chop the celery leaves roughly. Slice the shallot.

Heat the olive oil in a cast iron casserole and fry the shallot and carrot together. After 2 or 3 minutes add the fennel seeds and the celery leaves, stir to prevent sticking and when the shallot begins to colour add the prawns, red mullet, squid and stock. When the stock reaches boiling, turn down the heat and simmer with the lid on the casserole for 15 minutes. Season with salt and pepper and serve in the casserole at the table. Have plenty of good home-made bread to accompany this marvellous dish.

Calamari Fritti

FRIED SQUID

SERVES 4

2 lb/ 1 kg squid, to make about 1½ lb/ 750 g cleaned weight

flour for dusting

a generous quantity of olive oil for deep frying

salt and freshly ground black pepper

2 lemons

E ven though this dish is sometimes described as alla romana, it is common throughout Italy. For this recipe try and find the longer type of squid, as this will have more effect when it is cut into rings. It is cooked more or less in the same way as the fritto misto and the only slightly more tiresome element in the preparation is the actual cleaning of the squid. In the town of Camogli near Genoa a curious annual celebration takes place when local fishermen organize a fried fish festival. So as to satisfy the thousands of visitors who flock to the town on this occasion, the fishermen install huge frying pans in the market place that are 10 metres in diameter. Several hundred litres of oil are used to fry something like 1,000 kg or more of fish. The whole meal is totally free and, what is more, accompanied by some excellent wine.

METHOD

To clean the squid, first of all divide the animal by pulling its head and tentacles away from its tubular body. This body should then be stripped of its skin and of the internal transparent 'bone'. Cut away the head but keep the tentacles, which will also be fried. Cut the body into rings, cut the bunches of legs only if they are very long.

Heat the oil in a deep fryer or a high-sided saucepan. Flour all the pieces of squid well and deep fry, a large spoonful at a time, so that they don't stick together while cooking. Fry for only 3 or 4 minutes. Drain carefully on kitchen paper, sprinkle with salt and pepper and serve immediately with slices of lemon and a simple lettuce salad.

Polipi in Umido

BRAISED OCTOPUS

SERVES 4

1 ½ lb/ 750 g very small octopus, or small cuttlefish

½ lb/ 250 g onion, finely chopped

2 tomatoes, skinned and chopped

2 cloves garlic, chopped

4 tbsp olive oil

1 oz/ 25 g pine nuts

6 fresh basil leaves

1 small glass of white wine

In Naples octopus are called purpetielli and are cooked in a variety of different ways. The recipe that I am about to describe is one that is quite simple to prepare. Its success depends almost entirely on using very small octopus. I know that outside Italy it is quite difficult to find moscardini, a small type of octopus, but I recommend you to try and buy the smallest variety available, since the larger octopus require a very long cooking time and will still retain a slightly rubbery taste.

Cuttlefish makes a good alternative when octopus is not available.

METHOD

Clean the octopus (if they are the very small ones you will not have to remove anything). If you have cuttlefish, remove the bone and cut off the heads, leaving the body and the tentacles.

Heat the oil in a saucepan and fry the onions. When they become transparent, add the garlic and the peeled tomatoes. Cook together for a few minutes, then add the pine nuts and octopus; the heat must be quite strong for a further 2 or 3 minutes. Now pour in the glass of wine, cover the pan and simmer gently until the octopus is cooked. The small ones will cook in less than 10 minutes. Just before cooking is complete, add the basil leaves, salt and pepper. Serve with rice.

Stoccafisso alla Vicentina

STOCKFISH AS IN VICENZA

14 oz/ 400 g dried
stockfish: soaked weight
nearly 2 lb/ 900 g

2 pints/ 1 litre milk

4 tbsp melted butter

salt and freshly ground
black pepper

1 tbsp chopped parsley

W hereas in most of Italy, baccalà means salt cod, in Vicenza the same word confusingly means cod that has been dried without salt – in other words, stockfish. Like salt cod, stockfish needs to be soaked for a long time in water, which should be changed every so often, before it can be used. Before being left to soak, however, it has to be beaten with a wooden mallet in order to soften the flesh. You can nowadays buy it already beaten (and since it is popular in Greece, it can often be found in Greek as well as in Italian delicatessens). The resulting tasty dish is even more delicious eaten next day.

METHOD

Put the beaten stockfish completely covered in water to soak in a large bowl for at least 24 hours, even 2 days. Try to change the water three or four times during that period. After soaking, drain the fish, peel off the skin and tear the flesh away from the bones, breaking it up into shreds. Heat the milk in a large saucepan; when very hot, add the pieces of stockfish, turn the heat down very low and slowly simmer for 2 ½–3 hours. Stir the fish from time to time to make sure it doesn't stick to the bottom. The fish is cooked when it has totally disintegrated and absorbed all the milk.

At this stage, add the butter, stirring all the time, the salt, a lot of freshly ground black pepper and the parsley. Serve immediately with slices of grilled polenta.

POULTRY AND GAME

Pollo al Forno con Patate

ROAST CHICKEN WITH POTATOES

T his homely dish is known in all the regions of Italy. Chicken used to be a Sunday dish, but is now eaten on any day of the week. As this is an easy recipe which does not require much preparation time, it is highly suitable for a weekday meal.

METHOD

Preheat the oven to hot No 7/ 425°F/ 220°C.

Clean the chicken and cut it up into 12–16 pieces. Peel the potatoes and cut them into quarters, then slice the onion. Put the chicken pieces together with the potatoes into a baking tray, mix together with the sliced onion and the whole rosemary leaves. Season with salt and pepper and pour over the olive oil. Scatter the unpeeled garlic cloves on the top and place in the oven. After 20 minutes, turn the heat down to No 5/ 375°F/ 190°C. During the roasting time, turn the chicken and potatoes over occasionally so that they cook evenly on all sides. The potatoes should be golden and the garlic crisp after about 1 hour. Serve with salad.

1 roasting chicken weighing 3 lb/ 1.5 kg

2 lb/ 1 kg medium-sized yellow waxy potatoes

1 onion

2 sprigs of fresh rosemary

20 unpeeled cloves garlic

salt and freshly ground black pepper

10 tbsp olive oil

Pollo Farcito

STUFFED BONED CHICKEN

🏛

SERVES 6

1 chicken weighing 2 lb/
1 kg, cleaned

For the Stuffing:

2 oz/ 1 ½ US cups/ 60 g
fresh white bread
crumbs: include some
crust

4 fl oz/ ½ US cup/ 100 ml
milk

good 1 oz/ 2 tbsp/ 30 g
butter

1 small onion, sliced

½ lb/ 250 g field
mushrooms, sliced

1 clove garlic, chopped

1 tbsp finely chopped
fresh rosemary

good 1 oz/ 6 tbsp/ 30 g
freshly grated Parmesan
cheese

2 tbsp chopped parsley

salt and freshly ground
black pepper

3 eggs

T he most important thing in this recipe is to remove the chicken bones without cutting the skin. It takes some skill to do this, but if you use a very sharp knife and keep the cutting edge facing the bone rather than the flesh you reduce the risk of piercing the skin.

METHOD

First bone the chicken. Holding it with its breast downwards, slit the skin and flesh along the back-bone from neck to tail. With your sharp knife, work the flesh away from the rib cage on either side. When you come to the ball joints where the wings and legs join the carcass, cut through them and continue down either side of the breastbone. Lift the rib cage and free it by cutting very closely against the ridge of the breastbone – be especially careful not to puncture the fine skin here.

Cut off the two lower joints of each wing. From the inside, work the flesh off the bone and pull it out, turning it inside out in the process. Repeat for the legs.

Preheat the oven to No 6/ 440°F/ 200°C while you make the stuffing. Put the bread crumbs to soak in the milk. Meanwhile, heat the butter in a pan and fry the sliced onion and mushrooms for 5 minutes, then add the chopped garlic clove and stir-fry for a further 5 minutes to reduce any liquid. Remove from the stove and leave to cool.

In a separate bowl mix together the soaked bread crumbs, squeezed of any excess milk, the rosemary, grated Parmesan cheese, parsley and the salt and pepper. Beat the eggs and add them to the

bread crumb mixture and finally stir in the cooled
mushrooms, onions and garlic. The mixture
should be fairly dry in texture.

Heap the stuffing lengthwise along the centre
of the boned chicken, fold the skin up over it to
enclose it and sew up with a kitchen needle and fine
string. Place the bird in an oven dish with the
olive oil and bake in the hot oven, basting now and
again. Turn the chicken over for the last 15 minutes of cooking; the bird should take about 1 hour
altogether.

When fully cooked, let the chicken cool down
slightly before removing the string and cutting it
into slices. Accompany with new potatoes and
peas.

For roasting:
———
2 tbsp olive oil
———

Saltimbocca di Pollo

CHICKEN SALTIMBOCCA

SERVES 4

3 large chicken breasts

4 oz/ 100 g fontina
cheese

4 oz/ 100 g prosciutto
crudo (Parma ham)

12 sage leaves

1 ½ oz/ 3 tbsp/ 45 g
butter

salt and freshly ground
black pepper

T his is yet another extremely simple and eco-nomical dish which produces a good result. It is ideally suited to light lunches where the food is prepared immediately before eating. As this dish contains fontina cheese which dissolves on cooking, serve it without any delay.

METHOD

Cut each chicken breast into four diagonal slices. Flatten the slices by lightly beating them between sheets of plastic. Slice the fontina cheese into 12 pieces. Cut the prosciutto into pieces the same size as the flattened chicken slices. Now place on each chicken slice a piece of fontina cheese and sea-son with salt and freshly ground pepper and one sage leaf. Cover with the prosciutto.

In a large pan heat the butter until it fizzes, place the saltimbocca prosciutto-side-down into the hot butter and fry briefly, hardly for a minute, before turning them over. Continue to fry gently until you see the fontina has melted and the chick-en has cooked. Serve immediately, three per per-son, accompanied by the broad beans and bacon (Fave fresche alla pancetta) on page 109.

Supreme di Pollo al Limone

CHICKEN SUPREME WITH CAPERS AND LEMON

C hicken meat is very delicate and is suitable for almost any diet. This way of cooking it contrasts the tenderness of the breast with the intense flavour of the capers and the acidity of the lemon. This is an extremely easy recipe, and chicken breasts can be found anywhere.

METHOD

Season the flour with salt and pepper and roll the chicken breasts lightly in it. Put the capers to soak in a little water.

Heat the butter in a large pan and when it is hot, not brown, add the chicken breasts. Fry gently on each side until they are cooked and golden-brown – about 15 minutes. Remove the chicken to a heated serving dish. Now add to the same pan the capers (chopped into pieces if they are the large variety), the grated rind of the lemon and all its juice. Stir well to deglaze the pan, season with salt and pepper and pour over the chicken breasts.

4 chicken breasts

white flour for dusting

salt and freshly ground black pepper

1 ½ oz/ 3 tbsp/ 45 g butter

1 tbsp capers (salted if possible)

the grated rind and juice of 1 large lemon

Tacchino al Forno

ROAST TURKEY

SERVES 6

1 turkey weighing
6–9 lbs/ 3–4 kg,
including the liver and
giblets

4 onions

4 carrots

2 large sprigs of fresh
rosemary

8 tbsp olive oil

salt and freshly ground
black pepper

2 glasses of white wine

O ther people may consider this way of cooking turkey slightly sacrilegious. In Italy we not only roast turkey in the conventional way, but also cook it cut into smaller pieces. This is possible as Italian turkeys are usually of a smaller size than English or American ones. It is customary to eat this dish at Christmas as a complement to other meat dishes.

METHOD

Preheat the oven to hot No 7/ 425°F/ 220°C.

Cut the turkey into portions: cut each leg into 4 pieces and each breast into 8 or 10 pieces. Place all the turkey pieces, including the whole liver and giblets, in a large baking tray. Slice the onions and carrots and mix them together with the turkey. Pour over this the olive oil, sprinkle with the whole rosemary leaves and season with salt and pepper. Place in the oven. After half an hour turn the heat down to No 5/ 375°F/ 190°C, turn over the pieces of turkey and add the wine. Continue to roast at this lower temperature for a further hour, turning the turkey pieces over from time to time. The turkey should be cooked after an hour and a half, but you should taste for yourself in order to judge. Serve with the juices from the pan, accompanied by the Savoy cabbage with bacon (Cavolo verza con pancetta) on p. 111.

Petto d'Anitra al Mango

DUCK WITH MANGO

I t is quite usual to see duck accompanied by some sort of fruit – be it cherries, grapes, dates or, of course, oranges – in recipes that seem mostly to be of French origin. I do not wish to start heated discussions with our French friends, but le canard à l'orange was a dish served up in the Tuscan courts in 1600 – a fact upheld by several menus from that period.

I have preferred to use mango (all the better if it is not totally ripe), as it adds a touch of acidity to the duck meat which is usually rather fatty.

METHOD

Salt and pepper the duck breasts. Heat the first 30 g of butter in a heavy pan which has a fitting lid, and quickly fry the breasts, skin-side down, for 5 or 6 minutes. Turn the duck breasts over, add the stock, cover with the lid and cook for a further 10 minutes, lowering the heat slightly.

Meanwhile, cut the mango in two halves, peel off the skin and cut the flesh from the stone in thin slices. When the breasts are cooked, remove them from the pan and keep warm.

Put the pan back on a moderate heat and add the second 30 g of butter. Stir it well into the duck juices and add the brandy, the mango chutney and some salt and pepper. Cook for a moment, then stir in the potato starch, mixed to a paste in a little of the sauce.

To serve, cut the duck breasts slantwise into slices and arrange them on warm plates alternating with slices of fresh mango. Pour over a little of the sauce and serve with spinach and new potatoes.

4 duck breasts with their skin

salt and freshly ground black pepper

3 or 4 tbsp stock

good 1 oz/ 2 tbsp/ 30 g butter

1 large mango (not too ripe)

a further good 1 oz/ 2 tbsp/ 30 g butter

2 tsp brandy

1 tbsp mango chutney

1 tsp potato starch

Quaglie con Uvetta alla Grappa

QUAILS WITH GRAPPA RAISINS

SERVES 4

2 oz/ ⅓ US cup/ 50 g
seedless raisins, soaked
in a small glass of
grappa

8 plucked quails

salt and freshly ground
black pepper

2 tbsp olive oil

1 ½ oz/ 3 tbsp/ 45 g
butter

3–4 tbsp stock

1 tbsp chopped parsley

A little planning is necessary for this dish, as you should put some raisins to soak in the grappa a couple of days beforehand. (Unless, of course, you have some already made. This is extremely simple: all you need is a jar filled with seedless raisins and topped up with grappa.)

Quails these days are easy to find all the year round as they are now bred for consumption. They represent a light but elegant dish for people without much appetite.

METHOD

Put the raisins to soak in a small glass of grappa, if possible two or three days ahead.

Preheat the oven to No 6/ 400°F/ 200°C. Clean the quails thoroughly, and rub with salt and pepper both inside and out. Heat the olive oil in a heavy pan or casserole over a strong flame, and fry the quails until they become golden on all sides: this will only take a few minutes. Place the open casserole into the hot oven and bake the birds for a further 10 minutes. When the quails are cooked, remove them from the casserole and keep them warm. Skim away any excess oil. Put the casserole back on a high flame, add the butter and with a wooden spoon stir it into the juices. Remove the raisins and add the grappa to the quail juices and butter in the pan; allow to evaporate for a minute, then add the stock, stir to deglaze the quail juices and now add the raisins and the chopped parsley. Season with salt and pepper and pour over the quails.

Coniglio S. Angelo

RABBIT ST ANGELO

Normally I never give a proper name to a recipe as I consider the name should reflect the ingredients used in the dish. This, however, is an exception and is dedicated to a man who lived alone on an island facing St Angelo of Ischia and was renowned for preparing rabbit in an interesting way. I don't know if this man is still living as he was when I heard of him 30 years ago. I have tried to recreate as near as possible his recipe.

METHOD

Cut the rabbit into smallish pieces and try to take out as many bones as possible. Lightly salt and flour the pieces, then fry them in the oil in a deep saucepan so that every side is well browned. Next add the garlic, the roughly chopped tomatoes, rosemary, thyme and white wine. Add the basil after half an hour. Cook these ingredients with the lid on the saucepan over a moderate flame. Every now and again stir the sauce and add the rest of the tomato juice or some water if you find it is becoming too thick. It will be ready after about 1 hour. Season with salt and pepper and serve hot, accompanied by some fried courgettes (zucchini) and boiled new potatoes or polenta.

SERVES 4

1 young rabbit weighing 2 lb/ 1 kg when cleaned

flour for dusting

3 tbsp olive oil

1 clove garlic, sliced

3 or 4 ripe seedless tomatoes, skinned, or 1 large can peeled plum tomatoes drained of their juice

1 sprig of rosemary

pinch of thyme

1 glass of dry white wine

some fresh basil leaves

salt and freshly ground black pepper

SERVES 8

1 big hare weighing 4 lb/ 2 kg

flour for coating

8 tbsp olive oil for frying

For the marinade:

juice of 2 pink grapefruit

18 fl oz/ 500 ml Barolo wine

2 oz/ 50 g raisins

5 cloves

the grated peel of an orange

10 bay leaves

1 large sprig of thyme, 1 sprig of fresh rosemary

2 cloves garlic

1 tbsp honey

1 bunch of celery leaves

1 large carrot, chopped fine

1 tsp mustard

For the sauce:

1 oz/ 25 g dried ceps

good 1 oz/ 2 tbsp/ 30 g butter

1 small onion

2 oz/ 50 g prosciutto crudo

Lepre al Barolo

HARE IN RED WINE AND GRAPEFRUIT

L uckily the hare, proverbially known for its astuteness, is able to avoid being caught by swarms of covetous hunters eager for its skin, otherwise it would undoubtedly be extinct by now. As hare is similar to wild rabbit, the meat has to be marinated overnight, like other types of game. In the olden days the marinade used to be composed of a sweet and sour mixture, and this idea may still be appreciated today.

METHOD

Prepare the marinade and leave the hare (cut into pieces) to marinate for 24 hours.

Take the hare from the marinade and dry with a cloth. Dust with some flour and fry in the hot oil on all sides. Heat up the marinade. Remove the pieces of browned hare from the pan and deglaze with a ladleful of the hot marinade.

Place the pieces of hare in a cast-iron casserole and pour over them the deglazed juices and enough marinade to cover. Bring to the boil, turn down the heat and simmer gently for 2 hours, until the hare is tender. After 1 hour of cooking add the dried ceps, crumbled in your hand.

Meanwhile, to make the sauce, chop the onion finely and fry in the butter until it becomes transparent, then add the prosciutto crudo cut into strips. Take the pieces of hare from the casserole. Strain the liquid and add it to the onion and prosciutto; stir well and simmer for a few minutes longer, seasoning to taste. Pour the sauce over the hare and serve yet again with grilled polenta crusts.

Camoscio in Salmi

VENISON STEAK WITH WILD MUSHROOMS

T his is a typical dish of the Aosta Valley region where it is still possible to hunt deer with a licence that is rather hard to come by. In the rest of Europe it is much easier than in Italy to come across this king of the mountains; in America it is easier still.

The recipe requires that you marinate the meat for a long time in a rather complex marinade. This is to take away the too intense gamey flavour of the meat and to make it more tender. It is traditional to serve the venison with polenta, which turns it into a princely dish.

METHOD

Marinate the venison for three days before you are to cook the dish.

Take the meat from the marinade, keeping the marinade to add to the sauce later, and dry with a cloth. Lightly dust the slices with flour and then fry for 5 minutes in the butter until brown on each side, and put aside to keep hot. Then, in the same butter, fry the sliced onion and the smoked bacon cut into small pieces. Now add the sliced mushrooms and fry all together for a few minutes until golden, then add 2 glasses of the strained marinade, allow to bubble and reduce briefly. Add the venison pieces, coat with the sauce and serve with grilled polenta crusts.

SERVES 4

4 ½ in/ 1 cm thick slices from a venison leg or fillet, weighing a total of 1 ¼ lb/ 600 g

flour for dusting

For the marinade:

2 pints/ 1 litre good red wine

1 small onion, chopped

5 bay leaves

1 sprig of rosemary

2 cloves of garlic, chopped

2 carrots, chopped

2 celery stalks, chopped

1 sprig of thyme

5 cloves

10 juniper berries

1 tbsp split black peppercorns

salt

For the sauce:

1 ½ oz/ 3 tbsp/ 45 g butter

1 small onion, sliced

4 oz/ 100 g smoked bacon, chopped

¾ lb/ 350 g mushrooms, sliced

MEAT AND OFFAL

Brasato al Barolo

BRAISED BEEF WITH RED WINE

The Barolo, king of Italian wines, is supposed to give the maximum flavour to meat and other dishes. Piedmontese beef, full of wonderful taste and tenderness, combines perfectly with the wine, producing this outstanding dish.

3 lb/ 1.3 kg rump steak cut thick in one piece

good 1 oz/ 2 tbsp/ 30 g each butter and lard

METHOD

In a heavy casserole just bigger than the piece of steak, heat the butter and the lard together. When very hot add the steak and brown on all sides to seal in the juices. Remove the meat and put to one side. Fry the sliced onion, garlic, the split carrots and the celery stalks for a few minutes, then add the herbs, cinnamon, lemon peel and the Barolo wine. Stir well, deglazing the sides and bottom of the casserole.

1 large spring onion, sliced

2 cloves garlic, roughly chopped

1 carrot

2 celery stalks

small sprig of fresh rosemary

Now replace the steak in the sauce, season with salt and pepper and cover the casserole. Simmer very gently for 1 ½ hours. Turn the steak frequently so that it cooks evenly, and make sure that it is always covered by the sauce. Add a ladle of stock if necessary. When the steak is cooked, leave it to cool. Strain the sauce to remove the herbs, cinnamon, lemon peel and vegetables. (You may wish to reduce the sauce by increasing the heat and boiling for 5 minutes or more before adding the steak.)

2 bay leaves

1 sprig fresh thyme

5 sage leaves

1 cinnamon stick, 1 ½ in/ 4 cm long, or 1 pinch ground cinnamon

the grated peel of ¼ lemon

Very gently reheat the steak in the sauce just before serving with new potatoes and a mushroom dish – ideally the mixed sautéed wild mushrooms (Funghi Misti in Umido) on p. 116 – depending on the ingredients available.

1 pint/ 2 ½ US cups/ 600 ml Barolo wine

salt and freshly ground black pepper

a little stock (optional)

Polpettone al Sugo

MEAT LOAF IN TOMATO SAUCE

2 lb/ 1 kg minced
(ground) beef

6 oz/ 5 US cups/ 150 g
bread crumbs made
from stale bread

2 tbsp finely chopped
parsley

2 oz/ ¼ US cup/ 60 g
freshly grated Parmesan
cheese

salt and freshly ground
black pepper

4 eggs

oil for frying

For the tomato sauce:

1 onion, finely chopped

4 tbsp olive oil

1 clove garlic

2 large cans peeled
plum tomatoes

10 fresh basil leaves

salt and freshly ground
black pepper

I confess that I have had to telephone my mother on more than one occasion in order to gather the exact ingredients to make up this economical recipe.

I distinctly remember the tremendous satisfaction with which this dish used to appease our appetites when my brothers and I were young. It had two advantages: the sauce in which it was cooked provided an excellent dressing for the pasta which was served up as a first course. Then the meat loaf – cut into slices – appeared as a tasty main course accompanied by peas with ham.

METHOD

Mix the minced meat together with the bread crumbs, add the parsley, Parmesan cheese, salt and pepper and thoroughly mix so that the meat is well incorporated. Lightly beat the eggs and add to the meat mixture. The mixture should stick together and you can now form it into a large oval meat loaf. If you have difficulty in shaping the meat loaf and it is falling apart, add a few more bread crumbs to the mixture. (It is a good idea to fry a small meatball first to check the seasonings before you make the meat into a loaf.) In a large oval cast-iron casserole, heat the olive oil and fry the meat loaf until it is a crisp golden-brown all over and retains the juices of the meat inside. Take great care not to break the loaf as you turn it in the casserole. Set the casserole aside while you make the tomato sauce.

In a separate pan, fry the finely chopped onion in the olive oil. When the onion has become golden, add the garlic and fry only briefly before adding the tomatoes, drained of some of their liquid. Cook the sauce over a medium flame for ten minutes, stirring to break up the tomatoes. Season with salt and pepper and add the basil leaves.

Now add the sauce to the meat loaf, put the lid on the casserole and return it to the stove. Simmer gently for about 1 hour. Alternatively, you can place the casserole in a fairly hot oven No 6/ 400°F/ 200°C for an hour. While it is cooking, gently turn the loaf from time to time. Remove the lid after 30 minutes to allow the sauce to thicken. When the loaf is cooked you may use the rich tomato sauce to dress some pasta prepared in the meantime. The meat loaf should be allowed to cool for 10 minutes before it is sliced. Serve with the potatoes fried with garlic and rosemary on p. 115.

Bollito Misto alla Piemontese

BOILED MIXED MEAT FROM PIEDMONT

SERVES 8

1 ox tongue weighing
about 3 lb/ 1.5 kg
preferably one that has
been soaked in brine

1 zampone

1 boiling chicken
weighing about 4 lb/
2 kg

1 lb/ 500 g beef brisket

4 carrots

5 stalks of celery

2 medium onions

1 large sprig of rosemary

8 medium potatoes

salt and freshly ground
black pepper

mostarda di Cremona for
serving

his is perhaps the most famous of all Piedmontese dishes as it invariably figures in
most good Italian restaurants abroad. It is a classic autumn or winter dish.

In Piedmont there are many ingredients available for the bollito, such as calf's head and feet
which, when boiled, will become gelatinous. Make
sure to include the famous zampone (stuffed
pig's trotter). You can easily obtain this speciality
from any good Italian delicatessen, only be sure to
examine the 'sell-by' date.

METHOD

Clean the ox tongue of any excess fat and gristle.
Clean and wash the chicken.

Into a very large saucepan (big enough to take
the chicken, tongue and beef), put the ox tongue,
cover with cold water and bring to the boil. Skim
away the froth that comes to the surface every
now and again. Boil the tongue for an hour, then
add the piece of beef and the boiling chicken, the
carrots, celery, onions, rosemary and a little salt.
Continue to boil the meats together for a further
2 hours. The boiling chicken and the beef should
be tested to see if they are cooked after 1 ½ hours,
as it is important that your meats are tender but not
falling apart. During the final half-hour of boiling
add your potatoes.

In a separate saucepan boil your zampone.
The cooking time is usually specified on the pack-
age, and most zampone are precooked so that 20
minutes is sufficient. When the tongue, chicken
and beef are cooked, remove them from the

saucepan. Allow the tongue to cool a little before peeling off the skin. Allow all the meats to stand for 10 minutes before carving. Arrange slices of all the different meats on a large hot serving plate. You may ladle a little of the stock on to the serving dish to keep the meats moist. Arrange the potatoes and other vegetables with the meats and serve with green sauce.

To make the green sauce, put all the ingredients except the olive oil into your electric blender and mix until you get a thick paste. Then slowly add the olive oil, intermittently blending, until you obtain a beautiful thick sauce. The amount of oil used depends upon the size of your bunch of parsley. You may wish to add salt and pepper, but usually the capers and anchovies are seasoning enough.

In some regions of Piedmont this dish will also be served accompanied by mostarda di Cremona (crystallized fruits in mustard syrup). You can obtain this from many Italian delicatessens.

For the green sauce:

10 anchovy fillets

50 capers

1 ½ oz/ 1 ¼ US cups/ 40 g bread crumbs

1 large bunch flat-leaved parsley

1 clove garlic

2 tbsp wine vinegar

about 14 fl oz/ 2 US cups/ 400 ml olive oil

La Pizzaiola

BEEF STEAK WITH PIZZAIOLA SAUCE

SERVES 4

1 lb/ 500 g beef sirloin
steak cut from the bone
into 4 slices, each about
¾ inch/ 1.5 cm thick

1 medium can tomatoes,
chopped in the can
(Cirio make a brand
ready chopped)

4 tbsp olive oil

2 pinches of oregano

2 cloves garlic

flour for dusting

salt and freshly ground
black pepper

'La Pizzaiola' is another classic name together with 'alla scapece' and 'al funghetto': the words alone indicate the way a certain food is cooked. La pizzaiola probably comes from how the pizza-making woman would have cooked with tomatoes, garlic and oregano in olive oil. La pizzaiola sauce can equally successfully be served with fish such as swordfish and tuna.

METHOD

Salt the meat on both sides and then dip into the flour. Heat the olive oil in a heavy pan over a high flame. Fry the steak as you like it on both sides. Remove from the pan and keep warm. Slice the garlic and add it to the olive oil, reduce the heat a little and almost immediately, before the garlic starts to brown, add the tomatoes, oregano, salt and pepper. Stir and cook for 5 minutes, incorporating the meat juices into the tomato sauce. Return the steaks to the sauce, and let them soak up the flavour of the tomatoes for a minute before serving.

Nodino al Vino

VEAL CUTLETS WITH WINE AND SAGE

B ecause veal is considered a rather tasteless meat on its own, it is usually accompanied by either a herb or a sauce which will enhance the flavour of the dish.

The main virtues of veal, however, are its tenderness and the facility with which it is cooked. It is for this reason that most Italian restaurants have a variety of veal escalopes on their menu.

The chop or nodino of veal is a typical Piedmontese or Lombardian speciality. The best known is 'alla Sassi', so called because it originated in the Villa Sassi restaurant, situated in the hills of Turin.

METHOD

Salt the veal and dust with flour. Heat the butter in a large pan; when hot, put in the chops and fry over a medium flame until golden on both sides. This takes about 10 minutes. Now add the glass of wine, and allow to evaporate before adding the roughly cut sage leaves. Turn the heat down and cook gently for a further 10 minutes, if necessary adding a little stock to keep the chops moist. Season and serve with the juices from the pan.

Fennel prepared 'au gratin' (Finocchi gratinati) on p. 110 is an excellent vegetable to serve as an accompaniment.

SERVES 4

4 large veal chops, including the tenderloin

salt and freshly ground black pepper

flour for dusting

1 ½ oz/ 3 tbsp/ 45 g butter

1 glass of dry white wine

10 fresh sage leaves

2 tbsp stock (optional)

La Milanese

VEAL ESCALOPE (SCALLOP) MILANESE

SERVES 4

4 veal chops with their
bones, each weighing
7 oz/ 200 g

1 egg

60 g dry bread crumbs

4 tbsp freshly grated
Parmesan cheese

5 fresh basil leaves,
chopped

salt and freshly ground
black pepper

oil for frying

4 lemon slices for
garnish

The veal escalope Milanese is similar to the escalope Viennese in that they are both cooked in bread crumbs. The Viennese, however, is almost always served with a slice of lemon and a rolled anchovy, which is not the case with the Milanese.

In this recipe I have deviated slightly from the classical method of preparing the escalope Milanese by adding some finely chopped basil and some grated Parmesan cheese with the egg. This addition renders a hitherto rather boring dish more interesting!

METHOD

Flatten the chops, leaving the bone, and trim away the fat. Beat the egg, add the finely chopped basil, the grated Parmesan cheese and some salt and pepper. Dip each of the escalopes in the egg and then roll them immediately in the bread crumbs. Heat the oil in a large pan and fry the escalopes over a gentle flame. When the bread crumbs turn a deep golden colour take the escalopes out of the pan and serve garnished with a slice of lemon and a leafy salad.

Agnello al Forno con Patate

ROAST LAMB WITH POTATOES

SERVES 6

T his is a dish which does not require any side-dishes or other vegetables as it is a meal in itself. Even the cooking itself does not require much attention as it is entirely left up to the oven. Aside from this, it is an extremely economical recipe, as you may use the cheaper cuts of lamb. In addition to all these qualities, this dish is delicious.

METHOD

Preheat the oven to No 6/ 400°F/ 200°C.

Peel the potatoes and cut them into thick slices. Slice the onion. Place the pieces of lamb in a baking tray, add the onions, potatoes and the sprig of rosemary broken into 3 or 4 pieces. Pour over the olive oil, season with salt and pepper and then mix all together with your hands so that both the meat and the potatoes are evenly coated.

Place the baking tray in the oven and bake for an hour and a half. Half-way through cooking, thoroughly stir the ingredients so that the meat and potatoes brown evenly. Serve hot, taking care to give everyone equal portions of potatoes and meat.

2 ¾ lb/ 1.2 kg boned shoulder of lamb, cut into medium-sized pieces

2 lb/ 1 kg yellow waxy potatoes, peeled weight

1 medium onion, sliced

1 sprig of fresh rosemary

5 tbsp olive oil

salt and freshly ground black pepper

Spezzatino con Peperoni

PORK FILLET WITH PRESERVED PEPPERS

SERVES 4

14 oz/ 400 g pork fillet

1 oz/ 2 tbsp/ 30 g pork lard

3 tbsp olive oil

4 cloves garlic

7 oz/ 200 g large red bell peppers (preserved in vinegar, if possible), drained weight. Alternatively, 2 small whole fresh red peppers plus 2 tbsp red wine vinegar

1 dried hot red chili pepper, crumbled

salt and freshly ground black pepper

This is both a rustic and a ceremonious recipe. The slaughtering of the pig which is to provide food for the country families for months to come is usually celebrated in winter, when this activity takes place. It is somewhat difficult to explain to vegetarians the nature of this celebration, which smacks of a pagan rite! It is only natural that this ceremony does not weigh on the country folks' conscience, since it is a matter of survival to them.

METHOD

Melt the lard with the olive oil in a large pan. When very hot add the pieces of pork fillet and fry, turning all the time, for about 10 minutes. Slice the red peppers and cut the cloves of garlic into slivers. Add these to the pork fillet and continue to cook over a reduced flame for as long as it takes to cook the garlic. The preserved red pepper merely requires heating up: if you do not have preserved peppers, sliced fresh red peppers will take at least 10 minutes longer to cook. You will also need to add 2 tbsp of vinegar at the end. Season the meat mixture with the crumbled red chili, salt and pepper, and serve piping hot. The country folk would accompany this dish with some good home-made bread. I will leave it up to you to chance an alternative.

Costine di Maiale con Ceci

SPARE-RIBS WITH CHICK PEAS

SERVES 4

H ere is another rustic pork recipe which – although it could never feature as nouvelle cuisine – is tasty enough to be appreciated by even the most delicate of palates.

METHOD

Put dried chick peas to soak in a lot of water (remember they will increase their volume three-fold) for 24 hours. Strain the chick peas and add to a saucepan of boiling salted water. Boil gently for 1 ½ hours or until the chick peas are cooked al dente.

Take a thick-bottomed saucepan or casserole large enough to contain both the meat and the chick peas. Heat the olive oil in this pan and thoroughly brown the spare-ribs: this will take at least 15 minutes. Move the spare-ribs around in the pan so that they do not stick. Chop the garlic, the celery and the carrots and add to the spare-ribs. Fry very briefly, just coating the vegetables with oil, and then add the tomatoes and all their juice and season with salt and pepper. Cook the spare-ribs in the tomato sauce for about 20 minutes, then add the drained chick peas. If there is not sufficient liquid in the pan to cover the spare-ribs and chick peas, add a ladle of stock or tomato juice.

Cover the pan and simmer for 45 minutes or until the spare-ribs are cooked: the meat should be coming away from the bones. Add the basil leaves 5 minutes before serving. Home-made bread, as usual, is a good accompaniment to this whole-some dish.

2 lb/ 1 kg pork spare-ribs with plenty of meat on them

8 oz/ 250 g dried chick peas, or 2 medium cans of chick peas

3 tbsp olive oil

5 cloves garlic, chopped

2 stalks of celery, chopped

2 carrots, chopped

1 large can Italian peeled plum tomatoes

salt and freshly ground black pepper

a little stock (optional)

5 or 6 fresh basil leaves

Fegato Burro e Salvia

CALF'S (VEAL) LIVER WITH BUTTER AND SAGE

SERVES 4

1 lb/ 500 g calf's (veal) liver, cut into 4 slices

salt and freshly ground black pepper

flour for dusting

1 ½ oz/ 3 tbsp/ 45 g butter

12 fresh sage leaves

I don't know if this can be even described as a recipe, it is so simple. All I know is that it can be found in most Italian restaurants, for the combination of liver and sage is delicious.

METHOD

Season the pieces of liver on both sides and then dust with flour. Heat the butter in a large saucepan. Fry the liver slices in the butter: being tender, they will only require cooking for a couple of minutes on each side. Add the sage leaves once one side is cooked.

Broad beans and bacon (Fave fresche alla pancetta) on p. 109 are an ideal accompaniment.

Trippa alla Genovese

TRIPE GENOESE STYLE

A ll the different kinds of offal represent true delicacies for countries such as France and Italy. In Britain and the USA, however, fanatics of these dishes are decidedly less numerous, perhaps owing to the fact that many butchers do not sell offal directly to the public. They may be found, though, in the larger more specialized shops. Tripe (or busecca, as it is called in Milan) is a part of the cow's stomach. Before being sold it has been blanched to a creamy white by being boiled for a short period.

METHOD

Clean the tripe and dry it with a cloth. Chop the celery, shallots and garlic and cut the carrot into strips. Heat the lard and oil in a terracotta pot (one that has a lid) if you have one, otherwise a thick casserole is suitable. Gently fry the shallots, celery and carrot together, add the garlic and before it turns in colour add the glass of wine. Allow the wine to bubble for a minute and then add the tripe and the stock, cover the pot or casserole and simmer gently for at least 1 ½ hours (the tripe should be slightly al dente). Just before serving add the parsley, basil, salt and pepper. Serve in soup bowls with a generous amount of freshly grated Parmesan cheese.

1 lb/ 500 g fine-textured tripe

1 carrot

2 celery stalks

4 shallots

2 cloves garlic

1 ½ oz/ 3 tbsp/ 45 g pork lard

3 tbsp olive oil

1 glass of white wine

1 ¾ pints/ 800 ml stock

1 tbsp chopped parsley

5–6 fresh basil leaves

salt and freshly ground black pepper

2 oz/ ¼ US cup/ 60 g freshly grated Parmesan cheese

Rognoni di Vitello Trifolati

CALF'S (VEAL) KIDNEYS WITH GARLIC AND PARSLEY

SERVES 4

1 ¼ lb/ 600 g calf's (veal) kidneys

flour for coating

1 ½ oz/ 3 tbsp/ 45 g butter

2 cloves garlic, sliced

half a glass of dry white wine

salt and freshly ground black pepper

2 tbsp chopped parsley

T|he word trifolati originally indicated the addition of truffles (from the Piedmontese trifola, meaning truffle). As the truffle is a rare commodity the word has assumed a secondary, more popular meaning – denoting that something is fried together with butter, garlic and parsley.

This recipe is based on veal kidneys which are the tenderest of them all. Anyone fortunate enough to come by some truffles may add slices of these to the kidneys, thereby transforming them into a more sophisticated meal.

METHOD

Thoroughly clean the kidneys, removing all the fat and gristle from the middle. Slice them finely, then roll them in the flour before frying in the butter over a high flame. Cook these for around 5 minutes, turning constantly or stir-frying, before adding the sliced garlic which should also be lightly fried for a moment or so. Next add the white wine and the salt and pepper and reduce for a minute or so. Just before serving, sprinkle with the fresh parsley. Accompany the dish with potato croquettes or fried potatoes and a green salad or, perhaps, a vegetable such as spinach dressed with olive oil and lemon.

CHEESES AND SALADS

Pecorino con Fave Fresche

PECORINO WITH BROAD BEANS
(FAVA BEANS)

1 ½ lb/ 600 g pecorino

3 ½ lb/ 1.6 kg young and
fresh broad beans

I n Tuscany and Lazio, it is the custom to eat
this speciality as soon as the fresh broad
beans ripen. You need those small tender broad
beans that can be found in late spring and early
summer. Fresh pecorino, also called caciotta,
should be absolutely fresh, but pecorino with
peppercorns and slightly aged pecorino are also
suitable.

This dish makes an impromptu meal – it is
tasty and can be eaten when one has not much
appetite. It can also be eaten as an hors d'oeuvre.
The quantities used depend on how hungry you
are. I would say about 6 oz/ 150 g of pecorino and
a dozen or so bean pods are sufficient per person.
Of course, these should be accompanied by good
home-made bread and a glass of white wine or a
chilled young red wine.

METHOD

Cut the pecorino cheese into thick slices. Put the
broad beans in their shells on the table and let
your guests pod them as they eat them. If you find
them very small you can eat them whole.

Mozzarella in Carrozza

DEEP-FRIED MOZZARELLA

The imagination of the Neapolitans has gone so far as to put the mozzarella in a carrozza (carriage) – one of the symbols of old Naples. It is a very easy, tasty recipe if cooked with a good stringy mozzarella and eaten right away. It can be eaten as a first or main course served with a green salad.

METHOD

Cut the crusts off the bread so that each slice measures 4 × 2 ½ in/ 10 × 6 cm. Slice the mozzarella into 4 thick slices about ½ in/ 1 cm thick. Beat the eggs lightly and season. Dip the slices of bread on one side into the milk and then place a slice of mozzarella on the dry side. Season the mozzarella with salt and pepper and make a sandwich with the other slice of bread, milk-soaked side on the outside. Dust the sandwich with flour and then soak in the beaten egg. Heat the oil in a deep fryer, alternatively heat oil about ¾ in/ 2 cm deep in a pan. Fry the sandwich in the hot oil, turning it over if you are using a pan. The sandwich should be a nice golden colour, slightly crisp on the outside and the mozzarella filling should have begun to melt on the inside. Drain on kitchen paper and serve immediately.

SERVES 4

8 slices of thin white bread

7 oz/ 200 g fresh mozzarella (try to buy the Italian ones sealed in water in plastic bags)

¼ pint/ ½ US cup/ 100 ml milk

6 tbsp flour

2 eggs, beaten

salt and freshly ground black pepper

oil for deep frying – olive oil is best

Insalata Primaverile

SPRING SALAD

SERVES 6

3 oz/ 75 g radicchio

3 oz/ 75 g white lettuce

4 oz/ 100 g small
spinach leaves

1 small bunch of
watercress

1 small bunch of chives

2 or 3 sprigs of mint

1 small bunch of flat-
leaved parsley

4 or 5 tbsp olive oil
(virgin if possible)

the juice of half a large
lemon

salt and freshly ground
black pepper

The spring salad, in short, should be a mixture of vegetables: obviously all the things that can be found in abundance in spring – young red lettuce, the small shoots from perennial plants in your garden such as mint, chives, parsley, etc. If you cannot find these, then buy some fresh spinach. The only rule is that everything should be perfectly fresh.

METHOD

Wash and dry all the salad ingredients very thoroughly. Slice the radicchio and white lettuce into strips ½ in/ 1 cm wide. Leave the spinach leaves whole, but remove any long stalks. Cut the stalks off the watercress. Chop the chives into short lengths. Roughly chop the parsley and tear the mint leaves off their stalks. Choose a large salad bowl and mix all the leaves together in it. Make the dressing by mixing together the olive oil and lemon juice seasoned with salt and pepper. Only pour over the salad seconds before serving, so as to avoid the vegetables being 'cooked' by the acid in the lemon: even the freshest salad can be destroyed by being dressed too early. A delicious alternative to lemon juice in the dressing is balsamic vinegar (aceto balsamico) – a mild and sweet fragrant vinegar.

Verdure in Pinzimonio

CRUDITÉ WITH VIRGIN OLIVE OIL

N o one seems to know exactly where the word 'pinzimonio' comes from. The dictionary says it is a derivative of the words 'pinzicare' (sting) and 'matrimonio' (marriage)! In any case, this is a typical Tuscan recipe that brings together good fresh vegetables, Tuscan bread and the excellent virgin olive oil for which Tuscany is famous. It is a spring dish, to be made around May, when artichokes, celery, spring onions and fennel are at their best. It is an excellent way to start a meal, or is good as a simple snack.

METHOD

Wash all the vegetables. Cut away all the tough leaves from the artichokes and cut off their tops, slice in half (if they are large, slice into quarters). Remove any choke. Cut the spring onions in half lengthwise. Quarter the bulbs of fennel, removing any green stalks and discoloured parts. Split the celery stalks into two, lengthwise. Serve the vegetables in an earthenware dish (preferably standing in iced water). Make each person their own bowl of virgin olive oil, with 3 tablespoons of oil to 1 teaspoon of salt. Dip the vegetables into the oil and eat with the bread.

SERVES 4

4 small or 2 large artichokes

8 small spring onions (scallions)

2 bulbs of fennel

8 tender celery stalks

12 tbsp virgin olive oil

4 tsp salt

1 loaf of wholemeal bread

Insalata di Finocchio

FENNEL SALAD

SERVES 4

2 medium fennel bulbs
(they must be young
and fresh), about 14 oz/
400 g cleaned weight

4 tbsp virgin olive oil

salt and freshly ground
black pepper

A bulb of fennel is a very versatile vegetable. Not only is it excellent cooked, but in its raw state it is good for every sort of salad. For those who like it, all you need do is eat it simply with good olive oil and salt and pepper. In southern Italy, little whole sweet fennel bulbs are eaten at the end of the meal instead of fruit.

METHOD

Keep a little of the green part of the fennel to scatter on the salad. Slice into very fine slices lengthwise so that each slice is held together by the stem.

Lay the slices out on a flat plate, pour over the virgin olive oil and season with salt and pepper.

Insalata di Fagiolini alla Menta

FRENCH (GREEN) BEAN SALAD WITH MINT

W hat could be simpler than French (green) beans in a salad? This recipe can be eaten either hot or cold. It is important to have very fresh beans, without strings. The combination of the garlic and mint, along with the oil and lemon, gives a totally unexpected flavour.

METHOD

Top and tail the beans. Boil them in plenty of salted water and cook until quite tender. Drain. Finely chop the mint and the garlic. Then mix them with the oil, lemon, salt and pepper and stir into the beans. Mix well and eat hold or cold.

SERVES 4

12 oz/ 320 g cleaned French (green) beans

salt

1 clove garlic

3 sprigs of mint

4 tbsp olive oil

the juice of 1 lemon

freshly ground black pepper

Insalata di Cavolo Verza

SAVOY CABBAGE SALAD

SERVES 4–6

1 good crispy Savoy cabbage weighing 10 oz/ 300 g without the darker outside leaves

6 anchovy fillets in oil

4 tbsp olive oil

3 tbsp wine vinegar

salt and freshly ground black pepper

I n winter it is difficult to find fresh salad that hasn't been grown in a greenhouse. The Savoy cabbage, white and crisp, provides an ideal accompaniment to roast meat.

I remember as a small boy, stealing a beautiful cabbage from a near-by field. One friend went home with an excuse to fetch the oil, one for the anchovies and one for the vinegar. We had found an old casserole with a broken handle. Behold, our own winter salad, eaten on a roof behind a warehouse in the chilly afternoon sun.

METHOD

Peel off the darker green outside leaves of the cabbage and with a very sharp knife slice the heart as thin as you can. Avoid the stalk. Chop the anchovies into small pieces and then in a bowl mush them together with the vinegar. When a smooth consistency, add the oil drop by drop. Season with freshly ground pepper and if necessary a little salt, but remember the anchovies are already contributing salt. Pour this dressing on to the cabbage, mixing well together so that every piece of cabbage is coated.

Insalata di Fagioli Borlotti

BORLOTTI BEAN SALAD

U sually, this salad based on canned borlotti beans, is made with tuna fish and onions and is found in most Italian restaurants abroad. I prefer the Tuscan version with fresh borlotti beans that have just been cooked. Alternatively, use dried borlotti beans as long as they are not too old. The small amount of ingredients in this recipe aptly demonstrates that a minimum combination of flavours can produce a maximum result.

METHOD

If using the fresh beans remove their pods and boil in slightly salted water. Cook until tender – they take about 1 hour. If using dried borlotti beans, put them to soak in a large bowl of water for at least 12 hours. Drain and boil in fresh salted water until tender – they will take about 2 hours. When the beans are cooked, drain and, while hot, immediately pour over them the olive oil and vinegar. Season with salt and pepper and scatter with chopped parsley. Many people like garlic with their beans: crush one clove into some salt and add to the oil when dressing. Ideally, borlotti beans should be served with good Tuscan bread – wholemeal will do.

SERVES 4

1 lb/ 500 g fresh borlotti beans in their pods, or 7 oz/ 200 g dried borlotti beans

4 tbsp virgin olive oil

2 tbsp wine vinegar

salt and freshly ground black pepper

1 tbsp chopped parsley

1 clove garlic (optional)

Bagna Cauda

GARLIC SAUCE WITH CRUDITÉ

SERVES 6

10 large cloves garlic

½ pint/ 1 ¼ US cups/ 300 ml milk

20 anchovy fillets

4 oz/ ½ US cup/ 115 g butter

4 tbsp double (heavy) cream

2 red bell peppers

2 medium artichokes

2 fennel bulbs

2 carrots

4 celery stalks

When you eat bagna cauda don't make any social appointments for the day after, due to the effect the garlic has on your breath! It is a typical recipe from the Piedmont region, and is usually eaten in autumn or winter when the cardoon has undergone its first frost.

The bagna cauda is more than just a salad. It is a ceremony where friends participate and consume large amounts of good Piedmontese wine, which could be Barolo, Dolcetto or Nebbiolo. My sister-in-law taught me the trick of cooking the peeled cloves of garlic in milk in order to make it easier to digest, but still retaining its characteristic smell and flavour. The peeled cloves of garlic are cooked in milk before being used in the bagna cauda.

METHOD

Peel the cloves of garlic and put them in a small saucepan with the milk. Bring the milk to the boil, reduce the heat and simmer gently for 30 minutes or until the garlic is soft and beginning to disintegrate. Cut the anchovy fillets into small pieces and add to the garlic and milk. Cook together, stirring, to mash the anchovies with the garlic to form a paste. Add the butter in small pieces and stir until amalgamated. Remove from the heat and allow to cool a bit. Put the mixture through a sieve and then stir in the cream.

Wash and prepare the vegetables. Cut the red peppers lengthwise into strips ½ in/ 1 cm wide. Remove any seeds and pith. Remove the tough leaves of the artichokes and cut off their tops.

Slice each artichoke into halves and make six slices from each half, cutting away any choke. Cut the fennel into halves and slice each half into six. Peel the carrots and cut each one lengthwise into six long sticks. Cut the celery lengthwise, each stick into four. Fill a large bowl with ice. Squeeze a little lemon juice on the ice and arrange the vegetables on top.

Serve the bagna cauda warm in a separate bowl for each person. To keep them warm, use little table heaters. Other vegetables can be eaten with bagna cauda: celeriac, hearts of cardoon and Jerusalem artichokes, preferably served raw, though you may blanch cardoon and celeriac.

VEGETABLES

Melanzane e Peperoni Ripieni

STUFFED PEPPERS AND AUBERGINES (EGGPLANTS)

y mother was always good at making this recipe. I remember it was delicious in summer when the heat was intense and it wasn't so necessary to eat large quantities of protein. This dish was nearly always served cold, but still crispy on the top, and accompanied by plain bread.

She used to prepare more than was needed. This was greatly appreciated by my brother and I at around one in the morning, when we returned from our summer escapades to raid the fridge!

METHOD

Preheat the oven to No 6/ 400°F/ 200°C. Slice each of the peppers and the aubergines in two lengthwise. Remove the stalks and the seeds from the peppers, leaving a clean cavity for the filling. Scoop out as much as you can of the flesh of the aubergine with a knife, taking care to leave the skin intact. Chop the scooped-out pulp finely and fry it in 2 tablespoons of oil for 5–6 minutes, until it is soft. Remove from the heat and leave to cool.

Chop the tomatoes, capers, anchovies, garlic and parsley finely. Then take the bread crumbs, Parmesan and nutmeg and mix well with the chopped ingredients and the aubergine pulp, including the oil in which it was cooked. When it is well mixed, fill the aubergine and pepper shells with this mixture. Put 2 tablespoons of oil in the bottom of an oven dish large enough to hold the eight halves and arrange them in it.

Pour the 3 remaining tablespoons of oil over the stuffed vegetables and bake in a hot oven for around 40 minutes. Serve hot or cold.

SERVES 4

2 large yellow or red bell peppers

2 medium-sized aubergines (eggplants)

2 tbsp olive oil

14 oz/ 400 g ripe tomatoes, skinned and finely chopped

1 ½ oz/ 40 g finely chopped capers (salted if possible)

12 anchovy fillets

2 cloves garlic, very finely chopped

4 tbsp finely chopped parsley

3 oz/ 2 ½ US cups/ 80 g fresh white bread crumbs

2 oz/ 50 g freshly grated Parmesan cheese

3 grates of nutmeg

salt and freshly ground black pepper

5 tbsp olive oil

Carciofi in Umido

STEWED ARTICHOKES

SERVES 4

2 lb/ 1 kg fresh artichokes

the juice of half a lemon

14 oz/ 400 g onions

2 oz/ 60 g smoked bacon

8 tbsp olive oil

2 cloves garlic, sliced

1 ½ oz/ 40 g capers

salt and freshly ground black pepper

2 tbsp chopped parsley

I know it is hard to buy the small tender artichokes needed for this recipe although they are easily found in Italian markets. But just in case you are able to find one or two particularly tender ones, this recipe is ideal. It's strange, but it seems that in Britain artichokes are nearly always boiled or served with a vinaigrette or hollandaise sauce, and this is why the importers bring in all those big, slightly hard ones. I hope people start asking for the smaller ones, as more dishes can be prepared with them.

METHOD

Clean the artichokes, pulling off all the tough outer leaves. Cut off the tops and the stalks about 1 in/ 2 cm from the base. (If the artichokes are large, cut them in half and then in quarters, cutting away the prickly choke with a sharp knife.) Put the thus prepared artichokes in a bowl of water with the juice of half a lemon to prevent them from going black where you have cut them. Slice the onion finely and chop the bacon into matchsticks. In a medium-sized saucepan heat the olive oil, add the bacon and fry for a couple of minutes. Then add the onion and when it begins to colour add the garlic and the capers. Cook together just for a minute over a medium flame before adding the artichokes and a ladle of hot water. Season with salt and pepper and turn the heat down low. Simmer for 20 minutes or until the artichokes are cooked. Bigger ones take longer – up to 40 minutes. Add the chopped parsley before serving. This dish is excellent cold.

Asparagi Pasticciati con Uova

ASPARAGUS WITH SCRAMBLED EGGS

A good summer recipe using those lovely green asparagus tips with their own special flavour. Obviously, if you use the locally grown sort in season, it tastes better than the cultivated sort from who-knows-where. And if you add to all this good fresh farm eggs, it will be delicious!

METHOD

Peel the asparagus stalks, removing any woody bits. Cut into 2 in/ 5 cm lengths, putting aside the tips. Boil the asparagus in lightly salted water until tender for about 15 minutes, adding the tips 5 minutes before the end. Carefully drain and put aside. Melt the butter in a large pan and add the sliced onion, which should be fried gently until cooked through but not browned. Add the asparagus stalks (not tips) and gently heat – don't fry. Beat the eggs, season them with salt, pepper and grated Parmesan cheese. Raise the heat and add the egg mixture to the onion and asparagus. Stirring all the time, cook the eggs to a scrambled consistency, add the cream and serve immediately, with the tips arranged on top.

SERVES 4

14 oz/ 400 g fresh green asparagus (cleaned weight)

1 onion, sliced

12 fresh eggs

2 oz/ 50 g freshly grated Parmesan cheese

2 tbsp double (heavy) cream

1 ½ oz/ 3 tbsp/ 45 g butter

salt and freshly ground black pepper

Torta di Spinaci

SPINACH TART

SERVES 4–6

For the pastry:

7 oz/ 200 g plain white flour

3 ½ oz/ ⅓ US cup/ 100 g butter

up to ¼ pint/ ½ US cup/ 100 ml iced water

salt

alternatively 14 oz/ 400 g frozen shortcrust pastry, thawed

For the filling:

1 lb/ 500 g spinach

4 eggs, beaten

7 oz/ scant 1 US cup/ 200 g fresh ricotta

2 oz/ 50 g freshly grated Parmesan cheese

4 or 5 grates of nutmeg

salt and freshly ground black pepper

This type of dish, based on shortcrust pastry and vegetables, is ideal for picnics, or as a main course if eaten straight from the oven. You can also use frozen pastry which is readily available in the shops.

METHOD

Preheat the oven No 6/ 400°F/ 200°C.

Wash the spinach and cook in a little salted boiling water for 2 minutes. Drain, squeeze dry, and allow to cool.

Make the pastry by crumbling together the flour, salt and butter very lightly with your fingers. Add enough iced water to keep the pastry together and shape into a ball. Take a 10 in/ 25 cm flan tin and spread the pastry out directly over the base and sides of the flan tin with your hands, making sure you have an even thickness. (Roll out the thawed ready-made pastry if you are using that.) Trim the edges, prick the surface, fill with dried beans and bake blind for 10 minutes. Remove the dried beans.

In the meantime, chop the cooled spinach. Beat the ricotta cheese with a fork, add the beaten eggs, the grated Parmesan, the spinach, nutmeg, salt and pepper. Pour the mixture into the pastry shell, spread it out evenly and bake in the moderate oven for 25 minutes. When cooked, the tart should be golden on top and set.

Cappelle di Porcini Fritte
FRIED CEP CAPS

A s you probably know by now, I am a fanatical wild mushroom gatherer! So it is not difficult for me to find the ingredients for this recipe – all I have to do is go into the woods at the correct time: if the season is right, the woods are full of them. However, if you regard mushrooms with suspicion, it will be easier for you to use large cultivated field mushrooms. Even though the taste is not as good, you then need have no worries about poisoning!

SERVES 4

4 large cep caps, 4 in/
10 cm, or 8 small caps,
2 in/ 5 cm in diameter,
or large open field
mushrooms

4 tbsp fresh bread
crumbs

1 egg, beaten

salt and freshly ground
black pepper

4 tbsp olive oil for frying

METHOD
Clean the ceps by wiping rather than washing them. Beat the egg and season with salt and pepper. Dip the caps in the beaten egg and coat in bread crumbs. Heat the oil in a large pan and fry until the caps become light brown on both sides.

Bietole al Burro

SWISS CHARD WITH BUTTER

SERVES 4

1 lb/ 500 g Swiss chard,
with stalks

1 ½ oz/ 3 tbsp/ 45 g
butter

7 fl oz/ 1 US cup/ 200 ml
water or stock

salt and freshly ground
black pepper

Whenever possible, I try to avoid cooking vegetables in water and then putting butter on them. Instead, I prepare them in a way that conserves the vitamin content and at the same time enhances their flavour.

METHOD

Wash and cut the chard, including the stalks, into 1 in/ 2 cm thick slices. Heat the butter in a large saucepan, and when melted add the chard. Increase the heat and stir to combine the butter with the chard, then add the water and salt. Cover the pan and cook for about 7 minutes. This vegetable has a taste similar to spinach.

Fave Fresche alla Pancetta

BROAD (FAVA) BEANS AND BACON

This recipe, again, is only good if you can find the smaller fresh, tender broad beans. They are difficult to find, as the growers prefer to sell the bigger variety. The frozen ones need an extra minute or two of cooking time.

METHOD

Chop the onion and cut the bacon into matchsticks. Heat the olive oil in a saucepan and fry the onion until transparent, add the bacon and stir-fry together until golden. Put in the broad beans and the water and cook, covered, until tender: probably about 5–7 minutes. Broad beans like this make a good accompaniment for game and other strongly flavoured dishes.

SERVES 4

1 lb/ 500 g fresh broad beans (fava beans), podded weight, or 1 lb/ 500 g frozen broad beans

1 small onion

2 oz/ 50 g smoked bacon

3 tbsp olive oil

¼ pint/ ½ US cup/ 100 ml water

salt

Finocchi Gratinati

FENNEL AU GRATIN

SERVES 6

2 lb/ 1 kg fennel bulbs

1 ½ oz/ 3 tbsp/ 45 g butter

scant 1 oz/ 2 tbsp/ 20 g bread crumbs

salt and freshly ground black pepper

I t is a pity that this most delicious dish, very well known and appreciated in Italy, is hardly known abroad. It has a very distinctive flavour and can accompany both meat and fish.

Choose round, fat, firm bulbs of fennel.

METHOD

Wash and clean the whole fennel bulbs. Cut off the top stalks and the hard base, and cut each bulb in two lengthwise.

Preheat the oven to No 6/ 400°F/ 200°C. Boil the fennel halves in salted water for 15 minutes, drain and leave to cool a bit before slicing. Butter an ovenproof dish, slice the fennel into ½ in/ 1 cm slices and lay them in the dish, slightly overlapping each slice. Dot with pieces of butter, season with salt and pepper, and sprinkle over the bread crumbs. Bake in the medium hot oven for 15–20 minutes until brown and crispy.

Cavolo Verza con Pancetta

SAVOY CABBAGE WITH BACON

SERVES 4–6

B acon, especially if it is smoked, seems to give an excellent flavour to vegetables, and cabbage makes a perfect companion to it. Roast pork is well complemented by this recipe. It is essential to have a good firm Savoy with enough white in it, although the green parts are tasty.

1 lb/ 500 g Savoy cabbage (cleaned weight)

2 oz/ 60 g smoked streaky bacon

4 tbsp olive oil

METHOD

Slice the cabbage very thinly. Chop the garlic and cut the bacon into matchsticks. Heat the oil in a large saucepan. Fry the bacon, adding the garlic and crushed chili, for 2 minutes: the garlic must not brown. Put in the cabbage, add salt, pepper and the water. Stir to mix and then cook with the lid on for 10–15 minutes until the moisture has evaporated and the cabbage is cooked.

1 clove garlic, chopped

1 dried red chili pepper

½ pint/ 1 ¼ US cups/ 300 ml water

salt and freshly ground black pepper

Peperonata

STEWED PEPPERS

1 medium-sized onion

2 large red peppers

2 celery stalks, with leaves

4 ripe tomatoes

5 tbsp olive oil

salt and freshly ground black pepper

This is a typically Piedmontese dish based on peppers, tomatoes, onions and celery.

METHOD

Prepare the vegetables; chop the onion, dice the red peppers, slice the celery and skin and roughly chop the tomatoes. Heat the oil in a large frying pan. When hot fry the onion, and as it begins to turn in colour add the peppers and celery. Fry together for 2 or 3 minutes. Now add the tomatoes and turn the heat down so that you slowly simmer the vegetables until they are reduced and resemble a ratatouille. This may take 35–40 minutes. Season with salt and pepper and serve either hot or cold.

Peperoni Fritti con Aglio, Capperi e Aceto

FRIED PEPPERS WITH GARLIC, CAPERS AND VINEGAR

The most important feature of this recipe is the slightly burnt taste of the peppers (red and yellow if possible) which is obtained by frying the vegetables so that the skin is scorched.

If I was ever late coming home, I was always glad to find a dish of fried peppers in the fridge!

METHOD

Cut the peppers into strips. Slice the garlic and put the capers to soak in a bowl of water. Heat the oil in a large frying pan and fry the strips of pepper. The oil should be quite hot. Stir while frying the peppers: their skins should begin to scorch at the edges. Then add the slices of garlic and the capers, drained and dried before being added. While these ingredients are sizzling, add the vinegar and salt, stir well and let the vinegar evaporate for a minute. Serve immediately if you like, but an excellent dish cold.

SERVES 4–6

1 ¾ lb/ 800 g whole red and yellow bell peppers

4 cloves garlic

1 tbsp salted capers (alternatively capers in vinegar)

4 tbsp olive oil

2 tbsp wine vinegar

salt

Cavolo Rosso con le Mele

RED CABBAGE

SERVES 6–8

2 lb/ 1 kg red cabbage

3 ½ oz/ 100 g smoked bacon

5 oz/ 150 g leeks

2 oz/ 50 g pork lard or goose dripping

4 cooking apples

1 pint/ 2 ½ US cups/ 500 ml cider

10 whole cloves

1 in/ 2 cm stick cinnamon

salt and freshly ground black pepper

This recipe improves with being made the day before you wish to serve it. The flavours go particularly well with roast pork or goose.

METHOD

Peel the apples and cut into quarters. Wash and slice the white part of the leeks; slice the red cabbage into strips. Cut the smoked bacon into matchsticks. In a large saucepan heat, over a medium flame, the lard or goose dripping. Fry the bacon in the hot fat until golden, then add the leeks and stir-fry for a few seconds so that they absorb some of the fat. Now add the cabbage, turn up the flame and stir continually, coating with the fat, for 2 or 3 minutes before adding the apples, the cider, salt, pepper, cloves and cinnamon.

Now cover the pan and when it has come to the boil turn down the heat and simmer gently for 50 minutes to 1 hour.

Patate Fritte con Aglio e Rosmarino

FRIED POTATOES WITH GARLIC AND ROSEMARY

This is another wonderful recipe containing simple but effective ingredients. The combination of rosemary and garlic give an unmistakably Italian flavour.

METHOD

Cut the potatoes into cubes ½ in/ 1.5 cm square. Heat the olive oil in a large frying pan, and when hot add the potato cubes. Spread them well out over the pan, but do not stir-fry until they form a golden crust. Turn the potatoes over and add the unpeeled garlic. Fry together to brown on all sides. Just before the end add the rosemary, salt and pepper.

SERVES 4

1 lb/ 500 g peeled potatoes

8 large cloves garlic, unpeeled

8 tbsp olive oil

1 sprig of fresh rosemary

salt and freshly ground black pepper

Funghi Misti in Umido

MIXED SAUTÉED WILD MUSHROOMS

SERVES 4–6

1 ½ lb/ 750 g mixed
mushrooms – oyster,
field, ceps, hedgehog

1 small onion

1 large tomato

5 tbsp olive oil

1 sprig of rosemary

2 bay leaves

salt and freshly ground
black pepper

I cook this recipe every time I have had an unsuccessful mushroom hunt. I find that even the small amount of mushrooms I have gathered provide an opportunity to have a colourful, flavourful recipe, ideal to accompany autumn game dishes.

METHOD

Clean the mushrooms, wiping them rather than washing them if possible. Slice the onion and peel and chop the tomato. Heat the oil in a large pan, fry the onion and when it becomes golden add the tomato, the bay leaves and the sprig of rosemary. Cook the tomato for a minute or two and then add the mushrooms. Continue cooking for 20 minutes more on a low heat, stirring occasionally. Season with salt and pepper.

FRUITS AND DESSERTS

Pesche Ripiene al Forno

BAKED STUFFED PEACHES

4 ripe peaches

2 tbsp unsweetened
cocoa powder

4 macaroon biscuits
(amaretti), crumbled

2 egg yolks

2 tbsp sugar plus 2 or 3
drops vanilla, or 2 tbsp
vanilla sugar

1 tbsp pine nuts

A typical recipe from Piedmont where the peaches grow in abundance. For this recipe you need those lovely big ripe peaches with the yellow flesh. This dish can be made well in advance as baked peaches are excellent cold, but not straight from the fridge.

METHOD

Preheat the oven to No 6/ 400°C/ 200°C. Cut the peaches in two and remove the stones.

Scoop out some of the flesh from the middle of the peaches to make room for the filling. Mix the cocoa with the crumbled biscuits, the egg yolks, sugar, vanilla and pine nuts, blending well. Fill the cavities of the peaches with this mixture. Grease an ovenproof dish and put the peaches in it. Bake for 15–20 minutes. This excellent dessert needs a nice glass of Moscato d'Asti to go with it.

Pere Cotte al Forno

PEARS BAKED IN RED WINE

SERVES 10

10 conference pears

2 pints/ 1 litre dry red wine

10 oz/ 1 ½ US cups/ 300 g sugar

1 cinnamon stick, 2 in/ 5 cm long

a few cloves

the rind of 1 lemon

Another very easily prepared recipe using cooked pears which can be found in many Italian restaurants. My mother used to make it in autumn when pears are plentiful and when the first wine has just been pressed. She would always make more than was needed; apart from being a dessert, it was also something special for us when we returned ravenous from school. The alcohol in the wine disappears when cooked, so the pears can be given to children.

METHOD

Wash the pears and pack tightly, side by side, in a deep-sided ovenproof dish. Pour the wine over and add the cinnamon, cloves and lemon rind, then sprinkle half the sugar on the pears. Put into a cold oven and bring the temperature up to No 6/ 400°F/ 200°C. Cook, basting the pears every now and then with the juices. After 45 minutes sprinkle the remaining sugar on to the pears and cook for a final 10 minutes. Leave to cool before serving.

If too much liquid remains, reduce it a little by boiling it, then pour it over the pears before leaving them to cool.

Tirami Su

PICK-ME-UP

SERVES 4

1 egg yolk

1 tbsp sugar

½ packet (1 tsp) vanilla sugar

9 oz/ 250 g mascarpone cheese

6 fl oz/ ¾ US cup/ 170 ml strong black coffee

1 tbsp coffee liqueur (Kahlua)

10–12 Savoiardi biscuits

1–2 tbsp unsweetened cocoa powder

T his is one of my favourite desserts made from that killer of a cheese – mascarpone. There are many recipes for Tirami Su, which translated means 'pick me up' or 'lift me up', due obviously to the large amount of calories in it! I developed this recipe using only a few ingredients. The result is stunning, judging by the reaction of the customers in my restaurants.

METHOD

Put the egg, sugar and vanilla in a bowl and mix gently to a creamy consistency. Add the mascarpone and fold in to obtain a cream. Put the coffee in a bowl with the coffee liqueur. Dip the biscuits for a second or two in the coffee mixture, letting them absorb just enough to keep firm but not fall apart. Starting with the biscuits, arrange in four individual dishes alternating layers of biscuit and mascarpone, ending with mascarpone. Dust with cocoa powder and put into the fridge to set and chill.

Crostata di Ricotta

RICOTTA TART

T his tart is another cheese-based dessert with a superb result which my mother used to make from time to time as a special treat, usually on a Sunday. Ricotta is used all over Italy to make sweets. However, the ingredients and method suggest that this recipe comes from the south.

METHOD

For the pastry, work the butter with the sugar, sherry and salt to a smooth consistency. Add the flour and work to obtain a stiffish dough. Put aside, covered, in a cool place for 1 hour.

The candied peel, angelica and chocolate should all be chopped into very small pieces about ¼ in/ 5 mm square. Beat the egg yolks with the sugar until creamy, add the chopped lemon zest. Beat the ricotta with a fork until light, then add it to the egg mixture. Finally, stir in the candied peel and chocolate pieces.

Preheat the oven to No 5/ 375°F/ 190°C. Line the bottom and sides of a cake tin with three-quarters of the pastry. Pour in the ricotta mixture and spread it evenly. Roll out the rest of the pastry and cut into strips ¾ in/ 2 cm wide. Make a lattice top on the tart. Put in the moderate oven. Bake until the top starts to turn brown – about 30–40 minutes. Serve cold.

SERVES 10

For the pastry:

9 oz/ 2 ¼ US cups/ 250 g flour

4 oz/ ½ US cup/ 100 g unsalted butter

2 oz/ ¼ US cup/ 50 g sugar

4 tbsp dry sherry

a pinch of salt

For the filling:

1 ½ oz/ 40 g candied orange peel

1 ½ oz/ 40 g candied lemon peel

1 ½ oz/ 40 g angelica

1 ½ oz/ 40 g bitter dessert chocolate

2 egg yolks

5 oz/ ¾ US cup/ 150 g castor sugar

the zest of half a lemon, chopped

1 lb/ 2 ½ US cups/ 500 g very fresh ricotta

Torta con Nocciole

HAZELNUT CAKE

SERVES 6–8

scant 4 oz/ ½ US cup/
100 g butter

1 oz/ 3 ½ tbsp/ 25 g
flour

4 ½ oz/ ½ US cup plus
2 tbsp/ 125 g granulated
sugar

4 large eggs

4 ½ oz/ 125 g hazelnuts
(shelled weight)

4 ½ oz/ 125 g ricotta
cheese

2 tsp grated lemon peel

6 tbsp peach or apricot
jam

1 tbsp water to mix with
the jam

1 oz/ 25 g chocolate
menier, or bitter
chocolate, grated fine

Yes, I like sweets as well! Foodwise, I think of myself as an all-rounder, as any type of food gives me satisfaction and pleasure. This cake is irresistible: it is a richer variation of the Crostata di ricotta. I prefer to roast the hazelnuts before chopping them, as this gives a much nicer flavour.

METHOD

Preheat the oven to No 6/ 400°F/ 200°C.

Lay the hazelnuts on a metal tray and roast them for 10 minutes in the oven: they should become a light, golden colour and their skins should be loose. Let them cool, then skin and chop finely. Butter a 10 in/ 25 cm flan tin. Grate the rind of the lemon. Soften the butter and beat it well with 3 oz/ ⅓ US cup/ 70 g of the sugar, add the egg yolks and continue to beat: the mixture should be soft and foamy. Fold in the sieved flour. In a separate bowl beat the ricotta with a fork until it is light, then add the chopped hazelnuts and the grated lemon peel. Add this mixture to the egg yolk and flour. Beat the egg whites until they become stiff, and fold in the remaining sugar. Fold very carefully the ricotta and flour mixture into the beaten egg whites.

Spread this mixture into the flan tin and bake in the medium oven for half an hour. Let the cake cool a little, then remove from the tin and place upside down on a plate. Dilute the jam with a little water and spread evenly over the top of the cake. Grate the bitter chocolate on the fine grater over the jam surface so that you have a light sprinkling all over. Serve with Passito di Caluso.

Biscotti di Meliga

POLENTA BISCUITS

Makes 30–40 biscuits

7 oz/ 1 US cup/ 200 g
unsalted butter

7 oz/ 1 US cup/ 200 g
granulated sugar

10 oz/ 1 ¾ US cups/
300 g maize flour
(polenta)

scant 4 oz/ 1 US cup/
100 g plain white
(all-purpose) flour

salt

the zest of half a lemon

2 whole eggs plus 1 egg
yolk

eliga is the Piedmontese name for maize flour from which polenta is usually made. This basic ingredient is very common in Italy and one way to use it is in the making of sweets. For this recipe you will need a fairly coarse maize flour that can be found in any good Italian delicatessen. The recipe is very simple. These biscuits are usually found in Carmagnola, near Turin and also in the Aosta valley.

METHOD

Preheat the oven to No 5/ 375°F/ 190°C.

Combine the flour with the polenta and the salt, add the butter, cut up into small pieces and the lemon zest, and mix together to a soft breadcrumb consistency using your fingertips. Beat the eggs, yolk and sugar together and then mix into the flour and butter to obtain a soft sticky dough. Butter a large flat baking tin. Using an icing bag with a large nozzle, ½ in/ 1.5 cm diameter, squeeze out 'S' shapes, circles and dots. Don't put them too close to each other as they will spread a little when cooking. Bake in the medium-hot oven for 15 minutes. The biscuits should be a wonderful gold colour with a darker brown rim. They are very crumbly and delicious.

Zabaglione al Moscato

ZABAGLIONE WITH MUSCATEL

SERVES 4

4 medium egg yolks

scant 4 oz/ ½ US cup/
100 g castor sugar

6 fl oz/ ¾ US cup/ 170 ml
Moscato Passito

Zabaglione is one of the best-known Italian desserts. You will find this delicious recipe, based on eggs, in nearly every Italian restaurant, both in Italy and abroad. Marsala wine is normally used along with the sugar to produce the fluffy consistency. The use of a good Moscato Passito instead of Marsala gives it a fresh flavour. If you don't have a special round copper pan, you can use a round bowl standing in a large pan of hot water.

METHOD

Beat the egg yolks with the sugar until the sugar is dissolved. Add the wine and beat for a few minutes more. Put in the bain marie over a low heat, and using a whisk, beat until a firm, foamy consistency is obtained. Pour into individual glasses and serve with very delicately flavoured biscuits.

Struffoli di Napoli

NEAPOLITAN STRUFFOLI

I f Naples can't celebrate Easter without the pastiera, then it is even more unthinkable to celebrate Christmas without struffoli. It is a must. My mother used to make these for Christmas, and they were subsequently devoured by us. In many families they will be made as presents for friends and relatives.

1 lb/ 4 ½ US cups/ 500 g flour

5 medium eggs

3 tbsp granulated sugar

grated rind of a lemon and of an orange

a pinch of salt

METHOD

To make the dough, beat the eggs with the sugar, then mix in the flour, adding the zest of the orange and lemon, the salt and the alcohol. Knead well for 3 or 4 minutes, make into a ball and cover. Leave to rest for 2 hours in a cool place.

1 tbsp pure alcohol (if not available, strong vodka will do)

oil for deep frying

Take a little bit of dough at a time and roll into sausage shapes with your hand to a diameter of ½ in/ 1 cm. Cut the sausage into small pieces ½ in/ 1 cm long. Make quite a few. It is quite laborious rolling out these sausages and will take you some time.

For the caramel:

9 oz/ 250 g honey

scant 4 oz/ ½ US cup/ 100 g sugar

Heat the oil in a small pan so that the oil is about 1 in/ 2 or 3 cm deep. Fry the struffoli quite a few at a time in the hot oil until slightly brown, remove and drain on absorbent paper. Continue this way until all the dough is used up.

2 tbsp water

For decoration:

To make the caramel, use a heavy-bottomed pan and heat up the sugar and honey with 2 tbsp water until the liquid becomes clear. At this point, add the struffoli and the chopped angelica, stir carefully until all the struffoli are coated with caramel. Arrange on a plate in the form of a crown. Decorate with silver balls (not too many) and leave to cool.

2 oz/ 50 g angelica

1 oz/ 25 g silver balls

SOME BASICS OF ITALIAN
COOKING

It is usually best to put yourself in the hands of a good Italian delicatessen. Most important for the smooth running of everyday cooking is to equip your larder or store cupboard with the basic ingredients that will allow you to cater for even the most unexpected of guests with good grace.

Groceries that you should never be without include: olive oil, rice, pasta, dried mushrooms, canned tomatoes, anchovies (preferably salted), capers (salted), dried and possibly canned beans (note that beans and tomatoes are the only acceptable canned goods in my book), polenta and hard-grain or all-purpose flour, salt and pepper and garlic. For herbs, I recommend that you keep (fresh if possible, grow them if you can): rosemary, basil, oregano, sage and bay leaves. Coffee beans keep better than already ground coffee.

ANCHOVIES

As well as being eaten as antipasti, preserved anchovies are an important constituent of sauces and a flavouring for other dishes. They reach their apotheosis in Bagna cauda. The best way to buy them is in their salted form: Italian delicatessens sell them in bulk from large tins. Soak them for 30 minutes to desalt them before use. If at this stage you dry them thoroughly, you can preserve them in oil for your own store cupboard to use at any moment. When you buy them, the flesh should be pink and fresh-smelling; and choose medium-sized ones – the larger ones have a grosser taste.

BASIL

In Italy we consider basil to be the king of aromatic herbs, and in my view its culinary value is far superior to all the others. It has a refreshing and distinctive quality which can perk up and enliven even the simplest of tomato sauces and other dressings. It is, of course, an essential of Pizza alla napoletana, and combines with garlic to reach its sublimest moment in Pesto all genovese.

What a pity that this delightful herb can be found in abundance only in summer (though I know some green-fingered enthusiasts who increase its lifespan by careful indoor cultivation and parsimonious use). Dried basil is no substitute for fresh. There are two possibilities for preserving basil for use out of season. One is to preserve a good bunch of leaves in oil, to which they will impart their fragrance. The other method, ideal for sauces, consists of chopping the basil coarsely and incorporating it in a pat of soft butter, which is then frozen wrapped in silver foil. If you freeze the basil butter in a cylinder no thicker than a thin rolling pin, it will be easy to chip pieces off the block when the need arises rather than having to thaw the whole lot.

There is a third method, which is to preserve basil in the form of Pesto.

BREAD CRUMBS

Every bread shop in Italy sells good bread crumbs, fresh and dry: they make their own. Dry crumbs for coating should be of good quality – not the luminous orange crust that often covers frozen food abroad. They are easy to make by toasting bread in the oven and then putting the golden rusks through a food processor. If you must buy packets, try to find makes imported from Austria, where they also care about the quality of this product.

CAPERS

Choose salted ones rather than those preserved in vinegar, which retain their vinegar flavour. You will need to desalt them before use by soaking for 30 minutes in water. Try to buy smallish ones.

CEPS

Known in Italy as porcini, in France as cèpes; members of the genus *Boletus*. Most readily available dried; fresh in season in markets and stores.

EXTRA VIRGIN OLIVE OIL

See Olive Oil

FLOUR

The wheat grown in southern Italy, particularly Apulia, and on the plains of North America and Russia, is durum wheat, a hard-grained variety which when milled has a slightly granular texture as opposed to the softer powdery flour commonly used for bread-making and other cooking. Commercially made pasta must (in Italy) be made from 'pura semola di grano duro': you can check this on the label. Pasta made from this flour stands up to cooking very well, swells in cooking to increase its volume by over 20 per cent, and is also both nutritious and easily digestible. For making home-made pasta and gnocchi, you may be able to find this semolina (which naturally must not be confused with the semolina used in puddings) in any store specializing in Italian products.

On the other hand, to make the home-made pasta all'uovo, it is best to use Farina 00, a fine grade of soft-wheat flour which is available now from most delicatessens; it is also perfect for pizza doughs. It needs no extra sifting.

GARLIC

Indispensable in Italian cooking, a clove or two imparting subtle flavouring to countless soups and sauces, while greater quantities are responsible for the famous Bagna cauda and (with basil) Pesto alla genovese. In spite of its reputation in myth and medicine from the ancient Romans to the present day, one must not get carried away: garlic must be used above all in moderation, and at the right moment. If you are preparing a dish that needs only a hint of the flavour, you can chop a couple of cloves finely and leave them to macerate in some olive oil; strain this oil to use in your recipe.

MINT

Mint has its place as an excellent tea in North African and Arab countries, and is an institution in Britain in the sauce served with lamb. Italians generally attach less importance to it, simply sprinkling it raw over salads. It's a favourite taste of mine, however, and I perhaps use it more in my recipes than do most of my countrymen.

NUTMEG

A vital ingredient in many Italian dishes, particularly those containing spinach and ricotta, whether sweet or savoury. Don't buy ground nutmeg, always grate it freshly as you need it. This is why our recipes deliberately list among the ingredients the phrase '3 or 4 grates of nutmeg'.

ONION

Together with garlic, onions form the basis of many Italian sauces. While the cooking of garlic must always be moderate, even minimal (never must it be allowed to become brown or burnt), onions can be cooked even up to the point where they become slightly caramelized.

A trick to prevent crying while cutting up onions is to breathe only through the mouth, since the nerves that are sensitive to the smell are situated in the nasal cavity. Equally, if after slicing an onion you rub a little table salt on your hands, you will find that the pervasive smell disappears almost immediately.

OREGANO

The one herb that will keep well in a glass jar. This plant, closely related to thyme, has a minty flavour and can be found almost anywhere in the Italian hills. It is much beloved of the southern Italians, who use it mainly in pizzas, but also in dishes such as baked anchovies and meat cooked alla pizzaiola.

PARSLEY

Parsley is ubiquitous – the flat-leaved variety, whose flavour is richer and more pungent than the curly-leaved sort.

PEPPER

As with nutmeg, our recipes always state 'freshly ground black pepper', and that is what it should be.

POLENTA

Made from coarsely ground cornmeal. This is less popular in the south of Italy than in the north, where it is one of the best-known specialities and is particularly suited to the cold winter months. It used to be the staple diet of the inhabitants of the Alpine valleys, who ate it with local produce such as butter, milk and cheese. Polenta requires a lengthy preparation but modern techniques have worked miracles to produce various brands of quick polenta which can be prepared in only five minutes.

OLIVE OIL, EXTRA VIRGIN

The results of the first cold pressing of the olives, this oil is expensive and should be used parsimoniously – literally a drop at a time is sufficient. It is very green in colour, slightly opaque and is viscous rather than fluid. It has a very pungent taste, and the full quality of its flavour and texture is best appreciated raw, which is why it is recommended for salads and uncooked sauces, as well as for the famous fresella and pinzimonio.

VIRGIN OLIVE OIL

This is less green and more yellowish in colour, is runnier and can be used more generously. It is ideal for salads, mayonnaise and for general cooking purposes, but not for frying as the flavour is still too strong.

'PURE' OLIVE OIL

Successive heated pressings of the olives produce oils which are more or less refined and blended, and can be used in all types of cooking. If the oil is of good quality, the flavour will still be distinctive, but bland enough to be used in frying.

RICE

Vialone, Carnaroli and Arborio rice, indispensable for risottos, are grown mostly on the Pianura Padana, on the plain of the Po between the provinces of Vercelli, Novara and Milan. The main characteristic of the ideal risotto rice is the fatness and starchiness of the grain which enables it to swell to at least three times its original volume, while still retaining a firm al dente texture.

Rosemary

This plant is typical of the Mediterranean, but succeeds in growing almost anywhere. A twig will endow any roast with a distinctive yet delicate flavour, and will counterbalance fattier ingredients: but don't overdo the amount used. One of my (many) favourites is to add rosemary to potatoes and onions cooked in the oven.

Sage

Sage is a significant ingredient in one or two distinctive recipes: it is indispensable with calves' liver, for instance.

Tomatoes

The Italian 'pomodoro' meaning golden apple reflects the almost mythical veneration attached to this versatile fruit. When I first moved away from Italy and its cult of the golden apple used extensively in daily cooking, it was difficult to find satisfactory quantities of fresh tomatoes. However, I soon overcame my prejudice against the canned variety (for sauces, at least), provided that these are of good quality. Not all canned tomatoes are good. Look for deep red fruit, preferably of the 'fiaschetta' variety, which is plum shaped, meaty and has relatively few seeds. The surrounding liquid should be thick and not too watery. Ask for 'San Marzano' peeled tomatoes, named after the town in the province of Salerno where enormous quantities of tomatoes are grown exclusively for canning. Sometimes a can has 'with basil' on the label, when the herb has been added to enhance the flavour. Canned tomatoes are available already chopped up for use in sauces, but it is easy enough to chop them in the can with a long knife.

In the recipes the following tomato can sizes are used:

a small can	226 g
a medium can	420 g
a large can	780 g

Fresh tomatoes for sauces should always be fully ripened: canned ones are preferable to unripe fresh ones. Skin them (by immersing in boiling water for a minute) and deseed them. In the markets of southern Italy you can find a type of small round tomato with a tough skin; they are very sweet, meaty and juicy inside, and are among the best varieties for sauces.

For salads the Italians prefer a type of tomato known abroad as the 'beef' or 'beefsteak' tomato: a large, meaty kind which they delight in eating almost green, whereas I appreciate them better well ripened but still firm.

Dried tomatoes preserved in oil are now commercially exploited, and make an excellent antipasto.

There is even a sixth-concentrate paste derived from this product, which I personally find much to my taste, added in small quantities to sauces or simply served with a knob of butter as a dressing for cooked pasta. A labour-saving product is Pomí, a purée available in cartons.

TRUFFLES

These are a combination of all the smells and the tastes of the world put together. Indescribable. Something you either love or you hate. So intense and so remarkable and so completely different from anything that you know. White truffles, which grow around Alba and Piedmont, are more powerful than the black ones. You couldn't travel on a train with a truffle, so intense is the smell. It would disturb the other passengers too much – because it wasn't theirs.

I remember when I was little in Castelnuovo

Belbo I used to go out with the truffle hunter. It was very misty, around 5 o'clock in the morning. I can still see the old man, the little dog, the trees. Wonderful. The dog would get wild with the smell and would search all of us. Then all of a sudden he would locate a truffle. Immediately the old man would come and put the dog aside, and dig with a little trowel. The truffles grow in the ground by the roots of some trees. The best ones are those which grow near the hazelnut.

VINEGAR

Always use good-quality wine vinegar; it can be flavoured with herbs such as tarragon or rosemary. I particularly recommend balsamic vinegar, which is the concentrated must of wine aged for a long time in special wooden casks.

VIRGIN OLIVE OIL

See Olive Oil

ITALIAN CHEESES

ASIAGO

A semi-soft cheese from the Veneto region made in the high plain of Asiago near Vicenza. It is made from semi-skimmed milk, and has a fat content of only 30 per cent. Each cheese weighs about 22 lb (about 10 kg) and is matured for two to six months, becoming spicier with age. It can be eaten on its own and can be used for cooking.

BEL PAESE

Translated literally, bel paese means beautiful country. It was developed·in 1906 by Egidio Galbani to be produced in commercial quantities. The cheeses weigh over 4 lb (2 kg) and are wrapped in wax to maintain their freshness. Bel Paese is very creamy in texture, and pale cream in colour; it is made from cows' milk, with a 52 per cent fat content. It can be eaten on its own or used for cooking. Galbani also produce an excellent range of factory-made products.

CACIOCAVALLO

This hard cheese takes its name from the way it is hung to dry and mature – on 'horseback' over a pole. It is common in the south of Italy, as well as in the Balkans and in Hungary. It was already known in ancient Rome. Made from cows' milk sometimes mixed with goats' milk, its layered texture is similar to that of provolone, and its shape varies from oval to square. It has a pleasantly spicy taste if matured, and is sweet when fresh. It is eaten in slices or grated on some pasta dishes.

FONTINA

Fontina is made exclusively in the Val d'Aosta region. The genuine cheese bears a proper mark of quality with the inscription 'Fontina from the Val d'Aosta'. There are many imitations, but their quality and flavour do not come anywhere near the original, which is pale cream in colour and has a definite sweetness. Fontina is particularly good for cooking fondue and when eaten with good fresh bread. Each cheese is round and flat, weighs up to 33–44 lb (15–20 kg) and has a brick-red rind.

GORGONZOLA AND THE VEINED CHEESES

Gorgonzola is made from a base of stracchino, with the addition of the harmless fungus *Penicillium glaucum* which transforms it into the unique Italian blue cheese. It originated in the town of the same name, but nowadays it is made all over Italy. It has a 48 per cent fat content and a delicate buttery taste.

There are several variations. Apart from the sweet gorgonzola, there is a spicier, more mature one. The other erborinati – all the green- or blue-veined cheeses – are castelmagno, made at Donero in Piedmont; dolce verde which is sold in tubes; dolcelatte, especially popular in Britain; and lastly gorgonzola-mascarpone (also called Torta di San Gaudenzio), made of alternating layers of gorgonzola and mascarpone.

Gorgonzola has various uses, particularly as a

dessert cheese and in sauces for fennel, pasta and
polenta. Sometimes I mix it with ricotta.

This must be the fattiest cheese on earth: it contains 90 per cent fat. It is made from an extremely rich cream, slightly acid and whipped to an
almost solid but very velvety consistency. Because
it has a neutral taste it is used almost exclusively for
making desserts and to enrich sweet sauces. It is
also used in sauces for pasta.

MASCARPONE

My mother used to mix it with egg yolks and
sugar to perk me up after the rigours of school. My
own version of this is the recipe called Tirami su.

This versatile cheese used in many dishes for its
astounding melting quality was originally made
only from buffaloes' milk, produced mainly on
the plain of Aversa and in the area near Rome
called the Agro Pontino. The original version is
kneaded by hand while the whey is still very hot (a
process that gives the cheese its characteristic 'layered' appearance), and much more expensive than
the factory-made type produced in the north of
Italy from cows' milk. Although the cows' milk version is decidedly more rubbery in texture, it is
nevertheless popular.

MOZZARELLA

Various types of mozzarella exist, including
walnut-sized bocconcini, 'pleats' of varying sizes,
and the classic round mozzarella weighing about
7–10 oz/200–300 g each. Good mozzarella should
be very white and fairly elastic, and still be moist
when sliced (the freshness can be gauged by the
'tears' of whey that emerge). When it is cooked it
melts and goes very stringy. Mozzarella is an essential ingredient in pizza and Italians like to eat it in
its natural state, uncooked and seasoned with salt,
pepper and a trickle of olive oil, or in a salad with
ripe tomatoes and a few fresh basil leaves. It is
sometimes made into 'mozzarella in carozza' –
fried between two slices of bread dipped in beaten

egg – or a knob is put into the middle of potato croquettes, or 'suppli' (rice balls).

The use of mozzarella has grown enormously outside Italy, where it is often produced locally by non-Italian companies. Avoid the disgusting kinds made in Denmark and Belgium which bear no resemblance to the genuine mozzarella. The Italian type is exported in plastic bags which contain some liquid to keep them fresh. You should store mozzarella in the refrigerator, in a covered bowl of lightly salted water.

Also to be found in the markets and in good delicatessens is the smoked version of mozzarella, which is of a brownish hue and which is mainly eaten raw as an antipasto. I tried it on pizza with very interesting results.

PARMIGIANO REGGIANO (PARMESAN)

True Parmigiano Reggiano is produced between April and November from cows' milk coming from the provinces of Bologna, Reggio, Mantova and Modena. Laws defining the manufacturing techniques of the cheese are very strict and a detailed description of the product must be clearly visible on the label. Only when you see this name printed on the cheese can you be sure of having bought the authentic matured product.

This cheese, one of the most famous in the world, plays an essential role in Italian cooking: it is usually grated on to various types of dishes – pasta, risotto, polenta, soups, for example. But it can also be eaten in chunks on its own, accompanied by some good bread and a glass of mature red wine. Parmesan is also excellent eaten with pears as a dessert.

A crumbly cheese, Parmesan belongs to the 'grana' (meaning grain) family, contains only 30 per cent fat, and is high in protein. It should never thicken, curdle or go stringy when it is added to hot food; if it sinks to the bottom of the plate, it is not the real thing.

Grana padano is a similar but slightly inferior

cheese, industrially manufactured from milk coming from different regions outside the area where
parmigiano reggiano is made. It is less matured
than the real Parmesan, and therefore damper in
consistency. I suggest you buy this only when you
can't obtain the true reggiano type.

Both cheeses are made in circular shapes weighing 66–88 lb/30–40 kg and matured for at least
18 months. (In some famous restaurants in Italy,
minestrone is served in the hollowed-out Parmesan cheeses – as the soup is served the sides are
scraped with a ladle, and some of the cheese is
dissolved into the soup.)

Always buy both Parmesan and grana padano
by the piece and grate it when you need it:
prepacked grated varieties are not recommended.

PECORINO

Fresh pecorino (sometimes called 'caciotta') does
not keep, but the matured pecorino, which keeps
for some months, is used in the same way as
Parmesan, grated on special pastas.

It is made from sheep's milk, from which it
takes its name, in shapes weighing about some
4 ½ lb/2 kg. It comes from central and southern
Italy and two islands – Sicily and Sardinia. The two
regions which both produce and use the most
pecorino are Lazio (where they call the cheese
pecorino romano) and Sardinia (where they call it
pecorino sardo). The farther south you go, the
spicier the pecorino becomes. The Tuscan version
produced in Pienza, for example, is sweet and
mature, while the Sicilian and Calabrian ones
contain whole peppercorns and are very spicy.

Roman pecorino is probably the oldest cheese
produced in Italy, and it was served on the tables
of the rich and poor alike; it is similar to the Sardinian pecorino – pale, almost grey in colour, and
nearly always made in the characteristic round
rush baskets and then air-dried. In Sicily the cheese
is called 'canestro', after the baskets.

The Romans love to eat fresh pecorino together with very young broad beans and good bread – see the recipe for Pecorino con fave fresche p. 92.

PROVOLA, PROVOLINI, BURRINI AND CICCILLO

All of these semi-soft cheeses are very similar – they have a fresh, creamy provolone base and are pear-shaped. Burrini are provola cheeses with unsalted butter in the middle; this gives a particular sweetness to the cheese, which is usually eaten on its own. Each cheese weighs about 1 lb/ 500 g and is characteristically tied with a blade of straw.

PROVOLONE

The enormous pear-shaped cheeses covered in wax which hang from strings in Italian food shops are provolone. They come from the south of Italy and are produced in various sizes and flavours. The one most popular in the north is made with calves' rennet, is sweet-tasting and usually sold fresh, or no more than two to three months old. The cheese made with goats' rennet is spicy and suitable for maturing – the more matured it is, the spicier it becomes – and is preferred by people from the south.

RICOTTA

After Parmesan, ricotta is the cheese most frequently used in cooking. During a brief summer visit to Maratea in the province of Basilicata recently I had the good fortune to meet a friendly local shepherd willing to initiate me into the art of making authentic goats' milk ricotta. I was surprised to find that the process is very simple. First of all the cheese milk is skimmed to produce a full fat cheese (eaten fresh at this stage, it is called 'caciotta'). Then a small amount of fresh milk is added to the existing whey, which is then set to boil again. In no time at all small blobs of ricotta rise to the surface and are carefully fished out and put in the traditional basket or 'cestello', where they drip dry. A light cheese is formed, of exceptional taste and very low fat content.

Ricotta can be made with cows' and sheep's milk as well as that of goats, or from a mixture; the fat content varies according to the milk used, but is usually between 15 and 20 per cent. Ricotta is ideal used in many cooked dishes – crêpes with spinach, for example, and in ravioli. It is also widely used in desserts and cakes.

When you are buying ricotta, make sure it is absolutely fresh and use it as soon as possible, because it quickly becomes acid and therefore useless.

There is also a semi-fresh ricotta that is eaten as a dessert cheese, and ricotta salata, a derivative of pecorino, being made from its whey and then dried. It can also be made from goats' milk. It comes mainly from the south and is used grated on pasta. The flavour is similar to that of pecorino, but it is much less fatty.

STRACCHINO, CRESCENZA AND ROBIOLA

At one time these cheeses were made almost exclusively from the milk of cows fed on hay in wintertime when they had come down from their alpine pastures. Stracchino, for example, takes its name from the word 'stracchi' which in the dialects of Piedmont and Lombardy means 'tired' – perhaps indicating how the cows feel in the wintertime. Originally, the cheeses were made in winter when the cold conditions enabled them to be stored for a while. Nowadays, of course, this is not a problem and they are available the whole year round. They are very soft rindless cheeses and are sold in specially wrapped portions ranging from 4 oz/ 100 g to almost 9 lb/ 2–4 kg in weight. Their flavour is deliciously fresh and sweet with a slight hint of sharpness. Typical dessert cheeses, they reach maturity in ten days, and can be spread on bread or crackers, but have few uses in cooking.

TALEGGIO

Another cheese typical of northern Italy, probably the best-known one produced and distributed by the Galbani company. Each cheese is square, weighs some 4 lb/ 2 kg and is wrapped in a special paper to maintain freshness. It has a 48 per cent fat content and a soft, sweet flavour. It reaches maturity after only one and a half months, and is an ideal dessert cheese. I also use it in dishes where the cheese should not go stringy.

TOMA

Piedmont is famous for its toma, which is made from cows' milk in nearly every valley in the region. Each cheese usually weighs 4 ½–6 ½ lb/ 2–3 kg and is sold in various stages of maturity – the maximum being two years. Most of the consumption of toma is local.

Eaten fresh, it has names like paglierina, tomella and tomini.

TOMINI AND CAPRINI

As the name suggests, tomini are very small fresh toma cheeses. They are made from semi-skimmed milk and are round, about 1 ½ in/ 4 cm across and ¾ in/ 2 cm thick. They are eaten with freshly ground pepper, olive oil and vinegar. The best come from Chiaverano, a village near Ivrea; they are bottled in jars, with pepper, strong chili pepper, a few bay leaves and covered with olive oil, and can be kept for a long time. In Piedmont these tomini used to be called 'elettrici' due to their spicy flavour – they were given this name when electricity was first installed in people's houses. Nowadays progress has made its mark and they are called 'atomici'!

Caprini are the same as tomini, but are made with goats' milk and are more common in southern Italy and in Sardinia. The only type of this exclusively dessert cheese obtainable abroad is the one preserved in oil.

INDEX TO THE RECIPES